FAMILY COURT GUIDE FOR BRITISH COLUMBIA

Garrett Wynne, LLB

Self-Counsel Press
(a division of)
International Self-Counsel Press Ltd.
Canada   USA

Self-Counsel Press acknowledges the financial support of the Government of Canada through the Book Publishing Industry Development Program (BPIDP) for our publishing activities.

Printed in Canada.

First edition: 2003

Canadian Cataloguing in Publication Data

Wynne, Garrett N., 1945-
    Family court guide for British Columbia: a do-it-yourself handbook./Garrett N. Wynne.

    (Self-counsel legal series)
    ISBN 1-55180-431-X

    1. Domestic relations courts — British Columbia — Popular works.
2. Support (Domestic relations) — British Columbia — Popular works.
I. Title. II. Series.
    KEB195.W96 2003   346.71101'72   C2003-910005-7
    KF505.5.W96 2003

Self-Counsel Press
(a division of)
International Self-Counsel Press Ltd.

1481 Charlotte Road	1704 N. State Street
North Vancouver, BC V7J 1H1	Bellingham, WA 98225
Canada	USA

Contents

Notice to Readers

Laws are constantly changing. Every effort is made to keep this publication as current as possible. However, the author, the publisher, and the vendor of this book make no representation or warranties regarding the outcome or the use to which the information in this book is put and are not assuming any liability for any claims, losses, or damages arising out of the use of this book. The reader should not rely on the author or the publisher of this book for any professional advice. Please be sure that you have the most recent edition.

INTRODUCTION

This book was written for the purpose of providing non-lawyers with a step-by-step guide to Family Court in British Columbia. If you have unresolved problems associated with child custody and maintenance, or cannot afford a lawyer and do not qualify for Legal Aid, you may find this book of assistance. This book does not substitute for sound legal advice. If at all possible, you should try to hire a lawyer to act for you because a lawyer is much more familiar with the process than you will be. But if you simply cannot afford to hire a lawyer, then this book will help you get the assistance that you need from the Court.

Family Court is a division of the Provincial Court of British Columbia. In Family Court you *can* get —

- an order dealing with custody and guardianship of children,
- an order dealing with maintenance for children,
- an order dealing with access to children,
- an order dealing with maintenance for a spouse,
- a no contact order, and
- various orders supplementary to the above.

In Family Court you *cannot* get —

- a divorce order, and
- an order for division of matrimonial assets.

Divorce and division of matrimonial assets are matters that must be dealt with in Supreme Court.

There are two levels of Court in British Columbia that deal with family matters. Family Court is the base level and Supreme Court is the next level. This book deals only with procedures in Family Court. It does not deal with procedures in Supreme Court nor does it deal with appeal procedures. If you become involved in either a Supreme Court application or an appeal, a lawyer is almost always a necessity. The procedures in Supreme Court are much more difficult to follow and comprehend without legal help.

The good thing is that Family Court is an informal setting where judges expect to deal with lay litigants (i.e., non-lawyers representing themselves) on a daily basis. The judges will do everything within their power to demystify the process for you. However, it does help you to have a basic understanding of what you are trying to achieve and how you might get there. This book is designed to give you that basic understanding.

This book contains 12 steps. There is a Step 13 as well, but it is an explanation of what happens at a hearing. I hope you will not have to go that far and that you will need only some of the 12 steps.

The usual application is for custody, guardianship, access, and child maintenance. If you are the applicant, and you want help from the court, you need to use the following steps:

- Fill in and sign an application, either Form 1 or Form 2 (see Step 1).

- Prepare an affidavit in support and have it sworn (see Step 2).

- Commence the action (see Step 3).

- Serve the documents (see Step 4).

- Prepare for the hearing (see Step 6).

- Prepare and file the order (see Step 7).

The remaining steps are things that might prove to be necessary, which in many cases are not. Review the steps and, if necessary, follow them. Use Step 13, only if you have to.

Family Court is a division of the Provincial Court of British Columbia. Everything you can do in Family Court is set out in the Family Relations Act and in the Family Court Rules. I have not reproduced these documents in this book, but for those of you who have Internet access you can find the information from the following sites:

Family Relations Act <www.qp.gov.bc.ca/statreg>

- Click F in the alphabetical list

- Click Family Relations Act

Family Court Rules <www.provincialcourt.bc.ca>

- Click Family Matters Useful Links

- Click Family Matters

- Click Provincial Court (Family) Rules

1
How to Begin

Step One: The Application

All process in Family Court is commenced by an application. Form 1, Application to Obtain an Order, is the basic application form and it is reproduced here as Sample 1. This form is your request to the Court for help. All you need to do is fill in the appropriate spots so that the judge has some understanding of what it is you want from him or her.

In Sample 1, there are 19 numbered areas where you will need to fill in information. Beside each page of the form, there is an explanation of the corresponding numbers. Read the form, then read the explanations, and use the blank form at the end of the book or on the disk as your actual application.

The information at the top of the form is referred to as the style of cause. It identifies the court file number, the court location, and the names of the parties involved in the case. The party filing the application is the Applicant. The party who must respond to the application is the Respondent. All documents filed in a proceeding have the same style of cause.

You do not have to type this form. It can be filled in longhand, but be certain that it can be easily read. If you have messy writing, print and use block letters wherever possible. Remember, the judge does not want to have to try to decipher what you have written.

The only time that you do not use Form 1 is when there is already a court file in existence and what you are asking for is a change to an existing order. If this is the case, you use Form 2 (see Sample 2).

Sample 1
APPLICATION TO OBTAIN AN ORDER

Form 1 (Rule 2 (1))

APPLICATION TO OBTAIN AN ORDER

Court File No. _____ **1**

Court Location _____ **2**

In the Provincial Court of British Columbia

In the case between:

_____ **3** _____

(Applicant's name)

and

_____ **4** _____

(Respondent's name)

5

Filed by:

Name_____Date of birth_____(APPLICANT)

Address for service_____City_____

Province_____Postal Code_____Phone_____Fax_____

6

Notice to:

Name_____Date of birth_____(RESPONDENT)

Address for service_____City_____

Province_____Postal Code_____Phone_____Fax_____

IMPORTANT NOTE TO RESPONDENT:

If this application contains a claim for maintenance, you are required to file financial information with your reply. If you do not, the court may attribute income to you and set the amount of maintenance to be paid. The applicant has estimated your gross annual income as set out in item 3 below.

7 **I am applying for:**

[   ] custody   [   ] guardianship   [   ] access

[   ] maintenance for a child   [   ] spousal maintenance   [   ] parental maintenance

[   ] an order prohibiting the respondent from interfering with the child(ren) and/or

_____

(name)

[   ] an order restraining the respondent from harassing the child(ren) and/or_____

_____

(name)

[   ] other order *(specify)*_____

8 **1 — Orders and agreements**

Are there any court orders or written agreements between the parties concerning separation, custody, access, or maintenance?

[   ] No orders   [   ] I am attaching copies of all other orders

[   ] No written agreements   [   ] I am attaching copies of all other written agreements

2 — Children *(complete if you are asking for custody, access, child maintenance, or a restraining order)*

Name(s) of child(ren)   Birth date(s)

_____ **9** _____

_____

_____

_____

_____

SELF-COUNSEL PRESS — FCBC (1-1)03

INSTRUCTIONS FOR SAMPLE 1

1 **Court File No.:** Leave this space blank. When you take your completed form to the Court Registry, the clerk will fill in this number.

2 **Court Location:** Insert the name of the city in which you are making the application; i.e., Vancouver, Vernon, Prince George, etc.

3 **Applicant's name:** Insert your full legal name.

4 **Respondent's name:** Insert the other party's full legal name (probably your husband or wife).

5 **Particulars of Applicant:** Enter your full legal name, address, telephone number, and fax number (if you have one).

6 **Particulars of Respondent:** Enter the other party's full legal name, address, telephone number, and fax number (if he or she has one). If there is an item that you don't know, just leave it blank. Remember this is a self-help project. You are expected to know or to be able to obtain most of the information.

7 **Relief Requested:** Place a check mark beside each item that reflects what you want. If you want custody, check the box beside it. If you want guardianship, check the box beside it. Leave those items that you do not need to deal with blank. In the normal case, where you and your spouse have just separated and you have children, you are going to need to have an order for custody, guardianship, access, and child maintenance. You may or may not want to make a claim for spousal maintenance, and you may or may not want to make an application for a restraining order. Step 9 talks more about restraining orders. (See Sample 8 for the restraining order.)

Note: You can go to court now to get the basic assistance you need and you can always go back later for more help. You do not have to do it all at once.

8 **Prior Orders:** If this is not the first application to the court, you should attach copies of all prior decisions. If you have a written agreement (separation agreement), you should attach a copy.

9 **Children:** Enter the children's full legal names and dates of birth.

My relationship to the child(ren) is_____ **10**_____
The respondent's relationship to the child(ren) is_____ **11**_____
The present custody arrangements for the children are:_____ **12**_____
_____

(If applying for access) I am asking for access to the children as follows:_____ **13**_____
_____

3 — Maintenance *(complete if you are asking for child or spousal maintenance)*
The current maintenance arrangements are: **14**
_____

I believe that the respondent's gross annual income is $_____ **15**_____because
_____
_____

16 I am asking for: *(complete only if you are asking for child maintenance)*
[ ] maintenance in the amount set out in the Child Support Table for_____children
(number)
[ ] special or extraordinary expenses, as follows:
_____
_____

Information for Applicant and Respondent

If this application contains a claim for maintenance, you must complete Form 4, following the instructions on that form, if —
• there is a claim for spousal or parental maintenance; or
• there is a claim for child maintenance and one or more of the following applies:
  • You are the person being asked to pay.
  • The claim is for an amount other than the amount set out in the tables of the Child Support Guidelines.
  • There is a claim of undue hardship.
  • There is a claim for special or extraordinary expenses.
  • The parents have split custody (that is, there are 2 or more children and each parent has sole custody of at least one child).
  • The parents have shared custody (that is, each parent exercises access to, or has physical custody of, a child for not less than 40% of the time over the course of a year).
  • One or more of the children for whom maintenance is claimed is of the age of majority (19 years in BC) or older.
  • The person who is being asked to pay is not a biological or adoptive parent of the child but has acted as a parent to one or more of the children for whom maintenance is claimed.

You may also provide this financial information before receiving the respondent's reply, in order to avoid delay, if you believe that the income of a respondent from whom child maintenance is claimed is over $150 000 per year, or that the respondent will claim undue hardship, special or extraordinary expenses, or make a counterclaim for maintenance.

4 — Restraining Orders *(complete if you are asking for a restraining order)*
I am asking for an order prohibiting the respondent from interfering with or harassing the children and/or myself because_____ **17**_____
_____

Note to respondent: If you fail to file a reply within 30 days of being served with this application, you will not receive notice of any part of the proceeding and the court may make an order against you.

Date_____ **18**_____   Signature_____ **19**_____
(month, day, year)

SELF-COUNSEL PRESS — FCBC (1-2)03

Instructions for Sample 1 — continued

10   **Applicant's relationship:** Enter your relationship to the children (i.e., mother, father).

11   **Respondent's relationship:** Enter the Respondent's relationship to the children (usually the other parent).

12   **Present custodial arrangement:** Write a short description of the current situation. For example:

The children were in the joint care of the Applicant and the Respondent until the separation. The separation occurred on June 1, 2002. They are now in the care of the Applicant. The Applicant lives in a two-bedroom apartment with the children. The Respondent lives in a bachelor apartment.

13   **Access arrangement:** If you are applying for access, you may add a short description. For example, "I would like to see my children every second weekend."

14   **Present maintenance arrangement:** Provide a short description of the current maintenance arrangement, such as:

The Respondent is paying child maintenance in the amount of $375.00 per month on the 1st day of each month. There are no arrears of maintenance.

15   **Respondent's income:** Enter what you believe the Respondent makes per year. How do you know the amount? Explain how you know this. For example:

I believe that the respondent's gross annual income is **$25 000.00** because the **Respondent works as a labourer**.

The accepted measure of income for **employees** is the tax return. If you have access to your spouse's tax returns, get the gross income figure from his or her last return and insert it here. Keep the returns for the past three years, if you can get them, and bring them to court when you make the application. If your spouse is **self-employed**, it is a bit more difficult. His or her tax return will be based on a statement of income and expense from his or her business activities. Get that statement. The Court will review it and will adjust the income based on the legitimacy of the expenses shown.

16   **Maintenance request:** Fill in the number of children for whom you are asking child maintenance. You must ask for maintenance as per the Child Support Guidelines (see Appendix 1). It is extremely unlikely that the Court will consider any smaller amount, even if you ask for less. Look at the Child Support Guideline page that corresponds to the number of children you have and find your spouse's gross income. The proper maintenance can be easily calculated. For example:

Two children. Spouse's income is $25 000.00. Basic maintenance is $375.00/month.

You *may* also ask for extra maintenance to help you cover special or extraordinary expenses. Those expenses are child-care costs incurred by you because you work, medical expenses for the children for special items such as braces, and extra expenses incurred for school. You can only ask for help with expenses that you actually pay out. If you are compensated from some other source for the costs, you cannot claim them.

If you make a special expenses claim, you will have to file a Financial Statement (Form 4) (see Sample 7) outlining your income and expenses because the special expenses will be apportioned between the two of you based on your relative incomes.

17   **Restraining order:** Complete this section if you are asking for a restraining order. If the other party has been violent or abusive toward you or the children, you can ask for an order to keep him or her away. (See Sample 8 for more information.)

18   **Date:** Insert the month, day, and year.

19   **Signature:** Sign the application. You are now ready to file it with the court.

Sample 2
APPLICATION TO CHANGE OR CANCEL AN ORDER

Form 2 (Rule 2 (2))

APPLICATION TO CHANGE OR CANCEL AN ORDER

Court File No._____ **1**

Court Location_____ **2**

F.M.E.P. No._____

In the Provincial Court of British Columbia

In the case between:

_____ **3**
(Applicant's name)

and

_____ **4**
(Respondent's name)

_____

5 **Filed by:**

Name_____Date of birth_____(APPLICANT)

Address for service_____City_____

Province_____Postal Code_____Phone_____Fax_____

6 **Notice to:**

Name_____Date of birth_____(RESPONDENT)

Address for service_____City_____

Province_____Postal Code_____Phone_____Fax_____

7 **and to:**

[ ] Director of Maintenance
     Enforcement

[ ] Minister under the *BC Benefits (Income
     Assistance) Act*, the *BC Benefits (Youth
     Works) Act* or the *Disability Benefits
     Programs Act*

_____

IMPORTANT NOTE TO RESPONDENT:

If this claim involves an order for maintenance, you may be required to file financial information
with your reply. If you do not, the court may attribute income to you and set the amount of
maintenance to be paid.

SELF-COUNSEL PRESS — FCBC (2-1)03

INSTRUCTIONS FOR SAMPLE 2

1 **Court File No.:** Leave this space blank. When you take your completed form to the Court Registry, the clerk will fill in this number.

2 **Court Location:** Insert the name of the city in which you are making the application; i.e., Vancouver, Vernon, Prince George, etc.

3 **Applicant's name:** Insert your full legal name.

4 **Respondent's name:** Insert the other party's full legal name (probably your husband or wife).

5 **Particulars of Applicant:** Enter your full legal name, address, telephone number, and fax number (if you have one).

6 **Particulars of Respondent:** Enter the other party's full legal name, address, telephone number, and fax number (if he or she has one). If there is an item that you don't know, just leave it blank. Remember this is a self-help project. You are expected to know or to be able to obtain most of the information.

7 **Notice to:** Check the box that applies to your situation.

8 [ ] I ask that the attached order* dated_____be cancelled.
(month, day, year)

Or

[ ] I ask that the attached order* dated_____be changed to the following:
(month, day, year)

_____
_____
_____

Or

[ ] I ask that arrears of maintenance be cancelled or reduced as follows:

_____
_____
_____

9 Since the order dated_____was made, circumstances have changed as follows:
(month, day, year)

_____
_____
_____

Notice to respondent: If you fail to file a reply within 30 days of being served with this application, you will not receive notice of any part of the proceeding and the court may make an order against you.

Dated_____**10**_____   Signature_____**11**_____
(month, day, year)

_____**12**_____
(name of applicant's lawyer)

*"Order" includes a written agreement filed under the Family Relations Act (section 121)

SELF-COUNSEL PRESS — FCBC (2-2)03

Instructions for Sample 2 — continued

8   **Cancel or change order:** Check the box that explains what you are asking of the Court. Fill in the date of the order that you would like cancelled or changed.

9   **Change of circumstances:** Enter the date of the order and explain how the circumstances have changed since the order was made.

10   **Date:** Insert the month, day, and year.

11   **Signature:** Sign the application with your complete legal signature.

12   **Lawyer's name:** Include the name of your lawyer, if you have one.

2
Taking Action

Step Two: Supporting Documents
Affidavit in Support

In court, the judge acts based on the evidence on the record. Evidence is simply a statement of fact made under oath by one party or the other. For the purpose of a simple application, the easiest method of getting your evidence *on the record* is to provide a supporting affidavit. An affidavit is a statement made under oath.

As a bare minimum, you should provide an affidavit in support of your application in the form as set out on the following page. You will note that the affidavit has the same style of clause as the application does. It identifies the court file number, the court location, and the names of the parties.

The affidavit, because it is a sworn statement, must be signed in the presence of a lawyer, a notary public, or a commissioner for taking affidavits. If you do not feel comfortable taking this document to a lawyer or a notary public for signature, you can usually get it signed at the court registry when you file the documents. One or more of the officials at the registry will be *Commissioners for taking affidavits*. There will be a charge, no matter who you get this document signed by. That charge will be in the range of $30 to $50.

Financial Statement

If you are applying for spousal support or for child maintenance in an amount other than the basic amount determined by the Child Support Guidelines (see Appendix 1), you will need to provide the Court with evidence of your financial status. To provide the Court with this information, you will need to file a financial statement to show the court your income, expenses, assets, and liabilities. (See Sample 7 for an example of a financial statement.)

You do not need to file a financial statement if you are applying only for custody, guardianship, or access. In this case, your documentation will consist only of the application and the affidavit in support (see Sample 3).

AFFIDAVIT IN SUPPORT

AFFIDAVIT IN SUPPORT

Court File No. **[1]**

Court Location **[2]**

F.M.E.P. No. _____

In the Provincial Court of British Columbia

In the case between:

_____ **[3]** _____

(Applicant's name)

and

_____ **[4]** _____

(Respondent's name)

AFFIDAVIT

I,_____ **[5]** _____, of _____ **[6]** _____ in the Province of British Columbia

MAKE OATH AND SAY AS FOLLOWS:

1. I am the Applicant in this proceeding.

2. I have read the Application and the statements of fact made in it and verily believe that those statements of fact are true.

3. I make this affidavit in support of my application to the Court.

[7] SWORN BEFORE ME at_____)

in the Province of British)

Columbia this_____day of)

_____, 20_____.)

) _____ **[8]** _____

) Applicant

_____)

A Commissioner for taking affidavits

for British Columbia

SELF-COUNSEL PRESS — FCBC (3-1)03

INSTRUCTIONS FOR SAMPLE 3

1   **Court File No.:** Leave this space blank. When you take your completed form to the Court Registry, the clerk will fill in this number.

2   **Court Location:** Insert the name of the city in which you are making the application; i.e., Prince George, Nelson, Victoria, etc.

3   **Applicant's name:** Insert your full legal name.

4   **Respondent's name:** Insert the Respondent's full legal name (probably your husband or wife).

5   **State your name:** Enter your full legal name.

6   **City:** Insert the city or town you reside in.

7   **Commissioner signature:** Leave this area blank. A lawyer, commissioner for taking affidavits, or a notary public will sign and date it.

8   **Signature:** Sign your complete legal signature.

Step Three: Commencing the Action

Once you have completed your application, affidavit, and financial statement (if you are filing one); you must *commence the action*. You do this by taking your documents to the closest Family Court, handing them to the registry staff, and asking that the documents be "filed" or "issued." The registry staff will stamp the documents with a dated court stamp and give them back to you. They will insert a court file number in the upper right hand corner of the documents. That is your file number and it will remain the same throughout the proceedings. If you file any subsequent documents, you need to insert the file number at the top of the style of cause where it says "Court File No._____."

You need to decide how many copies of the documents you will have to file. You will need copies for the court, for you, for each Respondent, and for the process server to attach to his or her affidavit of service. Four would be the minimum amount of copies you will need, but you can make as many copies as you want.

3
To Serve or Reply

Step Four: Service

You now must arrange to have the other party served with the documents so that he or she knows what you are asking for and can file documents in response to your claim. The preferred method of service is personal service, in which the documents are actually given to the person against whom the claim is being made.

Note: Documents must be served on the other party by an uninterested third party. You cannot serve the documents yourself.

You must serve the following documents:

- Application
- Affidavit in support
- Financial statement, if you have filed one
- Blank financial statement
- Blank reply form
- Any other forms that you have filed with the court as part of the commencement process

The court registry staff may be able to give you the name of a process server. If not, then look up *Process Servers* in the *Yellow Pages*. Take or mail your documents to the process server you choose along with the name, address, and place of work of the other party. If you can, provide a photograph of the person to be served. The process server will charge you for doing this job. The cost is usually a flat fee of around $50.00 plus mileage, so pick a process server who is close to where the other party lives or works so that the mileage charges are not excessive. You may have to prepay this charge. The process server will serve the documents and will provide you with an affidavit confirming the documents were served (see Sample 4). You need to take this affidavit to the Court Registry and file it.

As an alternative, you may be able to have a friend serve the documents. The friend will have to swear an affidavit that the documents were served, stating when and where that happened. The affidavit will have to be sworn in front of a lawyer, notary public, or commissioner for taking affidavits.

Sample 4
AFFIDAVIT OF PERSONAL SERVICE

Form 5 (Rules 2 (5) and 9 (10) (B))
AFFIDAVIT OF PERSONAL SERVICE

Court File No._____ **1** _____

Court Location_____ **2** _____

In the Provincial Court of British Columbia

I swear or affirm that I,_____**3**_____,_____**4**_____
                                                (name)   *(occupation)*

of_____**5**_____personally served_____**6**_____
                          (address)   *(name of person served)*

on_____**7**_____at_____**8**_____with a copy of the following document(s):
       (date)   *(address)*

(Make sure a copy of each document is attached and marked with the correct exhibit letter.)

Exhibit "A":_____**9**_____
                                      (name of document)

Exhibit "B":_____
                                      (name of document)

10 The party served was identified to me in this manner:

[   ]   I know the person.

[   ]   He/She admitted to being this person.

[   ]   Other (specify)_____

11 SWORN OR AFFIRMED BEFORE ME   )

At_____, British Columbia   )
    (city, town, municipality)   )
on_____   )   _____**12**_____
              (date)   *(signature)*

_____
A commissioner for taking affidavits
for British Columbia

SELF-COUNSEL PRESS — FCBC (4-1)03

There will be a cost for this service. If you have a process server serve the documents, he or she will provide you with a completed affidavit of service.

As another alternative, you can in some circumstances serve the documents yourself. You can serve the documents yourself only if the other party agrees to file a reply and to show up in court when the matter comes up for hearing. Otherwise, the court will require you to serve the documents by a third party.

Keep in mind that the other party will probably not be happy to receive these documents. Do not put yourself or a friend in jeopardy if you feel there is any chance at all of the other party reacting in an inappropriate manner. Use a professional process server if you can.

INSTRUCTIONS FOR SAMPLE 4

1 **Court File No.:** Fill in the court file number, if you know it. Leave this space blank, if you don't know the number. When you take your completed form to the Court Registry, the clerk will fill in the number.

2 **Court Location:** Insert the name of the city; i.e.; Vancouver, Vernon, Prince George, etc.

3 **Name:** The process server will insert his or her full legal name.

4 **Occupation:** The process server will insert his or her occupation.

5 **Address:** The process server will enter his or her complete address.

6 **Name of person served:** Enter the full legal name of the person served.

7 **Date:** Insert the month, day, and year the person was served.

8 **Address:** Enter the address at which the person was served.

9 **Name of documents:** Insert the names of the documents that are being served: i.e., Exhibit "A": Application; Exhibit "B": Financial Statement. Insert as many exhibits as needed. Make sure a copy of each document is attached and marked with the correct exhibit letter.

10 **Identify the party:** The process server must explain how he or she identified the person being served.

11 **Swearing the document:** A commissioner for taking affidavits, notary public, or lawyer will fill in the date, city, and his or her signature.

12 **Signature:** The process server needs to sign here in the presence of a notary public, lawyer, or commissioner for taking affidavits.

Step Five: Reply

If you are the party who is served with an application and there is a claim against you that you do not consent to, then you need to file a reply by filling in the form and filing it at the court registry from which the application was issued. You must file the reply within 30 days (see Sample 5).

Form 3 (Rule 3 (1) and (5))

REPLY

Court File No._____ **1**

Court Location_____ **2**

In the Provincial Court of British Columbia

In the case between:

_____ **3** _____

(name)

and

_____ **4** _____

(name)

_____

5 To:

Name_____Date of birth_____(APPLICANT)

Address for service_____City_____

Province_____Postal Code_____Phone_____Fax_____

6 From:

Name_____Date of birth_____(RESPONDENT)

Address for service_____City_____

Province_____Postal Code_____Phone_____Fax_____

_____

IMPORTANT NOTE TO APPLICANT:

If the respondent's reply includes a claim for maintenance, and you (the original applicant) do not file the required financial information with your reply, the court may attribute income to you and set the amount of maintenance to be paid. The respondent has estimated your gross annual income as set out in item 2 below.

7 Agreement with application:

I agree with the request(s) of the applicant for:

[ ] custody   [ ] guardianship   [ ] access

[ ] maintenance for a child   [ ] spousal maintenance   [ ] parental maintenance

[ ] a change in or cancellation of an earlier order

[ ] other order *(specify)*_____

I wish to make the following comments regarding the request(s) even though I agree:

_____
_____
_____
_____
_____
_____
_____

SELF-COUNSEL PRESS — FCBC (5-1)03

INSTRUCTIONS FOR SAMPLE 5

1   **Court File No:** Leave this space blank. When you take your completed form to the Court Registry, the clerk will fill in this number.

2   **Court Location:** The court location must be that of the one at which the application was issued. Insert the name of the city in which you are making the reply; i.e., Vancouver, Vernon, Victoria, etc.

3   **Applicant's name:** Insert the other party's full legal name.

4   **Respondent's name:** Insert your full legal name.

5   **Particulars of Applicant:** Enter the other party's full legal name, address, telephone number, and fax number (if he or she has one). If there is an item that you don't know, just leave it blank.

6   **Particulars of Respondent:** Enter your full legal name, address, telephone number, and fax number (if you have one).

7   **Agreement with Application:** If you agree with the application, you can check the box or boxes that apply and you can insert an explanation of anything that you want the court to know. For example, even though you agree that the Applicant should have custody and guardianship, you may want to explain to the Court exactly what you want in the form of access.

8 **Disagreement with application:**
I disagree with the request(s) of the applicant for:

[ ] custody   [ ] guardianship   [ ] access

[ ] maintenance for a child   [ ] spousal maintenance   [ ] parental maintenance

[ ] a change in or cancellation of an earlier order

[ ] other order *(specify)*_____

I disagree because:

_____

_____

_____

_____

_____

Respondent's own application

9 I wish to make an application for the following:

[ ] custody   [ ] guardianship   [ ] access

[ ] maintenance for a child   [ ] spousal maintenance   [ ] parental maintenance

[ ] a change in or cancellation of an earlier order

[ ] an order that arrears under the *Family Relations Act* be cancelled or reduced

[ ] other order *(specify)*_____

1 — Children *(complete if you are asking for custody, access, or child maintenance)*

Name(s) of child(ren)   **10**   Birth date(s)

_____

_____

_____

(If applying for access) I am asking for access to the children as follows: _____ **11** _____

_____

2 — Maintenance *(complete if you are asking for child or spousal maintenance)*

I believe that the applicant's gross annual income is $_____ **12** _____ because_____

_____

3 — Restraining Order *(complete if you are asking for a restraining order)*

I am asking for an order prohibiting the applicant from interfering with or harassing the children and/
or myself because_____ **13** _____

_____

Dated_____ **14** _____   Signature_____ **15** _____
      (date)

SELF-COUNSEL PRESS — FCBC (5-2)03

8   **Disagreement with application:** If you disagree with the application, you can check the box or boxes of requests such as custody, access, guardianship, etc. You should give an explanation of why you disagree. For example, if you want custody of the children, explain why you think the children would be better off living with you.

9   **Respondent's own application:** Check the box or boxes of the things you would like to apply for.

10   **Children:** Insert the full legal names and birth dates of the children.

11   **Applying for access:** You must insert a short explanation of exactly what access you are prepared to let the applicant have to the children or what access you would like to have to the children.

12   **Maintenance:** Insert what you believe the applicant's income to be and the basis of that belief.

13   **Restraining Order:** If you are asking for a restraining order for yourself and/or your children, you must insert a short explanation of why.

14   **Date:** Insert the month, day, and year the form is signed and filed.

15   **Signature:** Sign your complete legal signature.

    Note: If there is a claim against you in the application for maintenance, you must prepare and file a financial statement in addition to your reply and you must do so within 30 days (see Sample 7 for financial statement).

Attending Court and the Judge's Order

Step Six: Preparation for Hearing

Once you have issued and served the documents, the court will automatically set a date for you to come to court. The other party has 30 days to file a reply to your claim. The court date will be set after the 30 days. The proceeding will vary, depending on where you live and with which court registry you have filed the documents. In some courts, you will first receive a notice to see a Family Justice Counsellor. In other courts, you will simply receive a notice to attend at court before the judge on a particular date. In either case, you should keep the following things in mind:

- The court will always try to make the decision that is best for the children.

- It is almost never in the best interest of the children to be denied access to one or both parents.

- Whether you like it or not, you and the other party are parents and are going to have to figure out some way to interact with each other for a long time to come. Do not badmouth the other parent in front of the children.

- The children are going to live with one of you and are going to visit the other. The parent who has the children most of the time will receive financial assistance from the other parent in the form of child maintenance. Except in the most unusual situations there is no other possible result.

- Whenever possible, and this means almost all the time, you are better off to reach an agreement with the other party than to have the court impose an agreement on you.

Before you go to any hearing, spend some time thinking about why it is that what you want is better for the children than what the other party wants. Think about why you should not agree to what he or she wants. Get yourself into a position where you are prepared to negotiate a solution. Do not make the court do it for you.

The Family Court system is set up on a non-adversarial or co-operative basis. What the court wants you to do is to reach a consensus, an agreement, something you can all live with and live by. The court will give you a number of chances to do that.

If you are in a "Family Justice Registry," the first hearing will be in front of a Family Justice Counsellor. The counsellor will try to get you to settle your differences and he or she will point out to both of you what other services might be available to assist you in reaching a settlement.

If you are in a court registry that is not designated as a Family Justice Registry, the first hearing will be in front of a judge. The judge will try to get you to settle your differences and he or she will point out to both of you what other services might be available to assist you in reaching a settlement. The judge may not have the time to do that on the day of the first appearance; instead he or she will order a "family case conference" for that purpose.

If your first hearing is in front of a judge, you will have to wait your turn. When your case is called, stand up and identify yourself. The judge will likely ask you to come forward. Do so and address the judge as "Your Honour." When asked what it is that you want, tell the judge (e.g., "Your Honour, I want custody, guardianship, and child maintenance. I agree that the Respondent should have access."). Tell the judge that you are prepared to go to a family case conference if necessary.

The judge will then ask the Respondent what he or she wants. Just listen and do not interrupt. If the judge asks you a question, give him or her the answer. Remember to refer to the judge as "Your Honour" and do not ramble.

If the judge is of the opinion that he or she will be able to resolve the matter quickly, he or she may do so on the spot. If the judge decides that it might take some time to examine and discuss the disagreements between you and the other party, he or she will order a case conference. If the judge does order a case conference, you simply leave and the court registry will tell you when the conference will happen.

A case conference is an informal setting. You, the Respondent, and the judge have a discussion about the issues between you and the other party and what is best for the children. The judge will act as mediator. He or she will try to get you to agree on a settlement. In most cases, a settlement is exactly what happens. You settle the matter, and it is over.

If you are not able to settle matters by this time, the court will order that the matter be set for hearing. You want to avoid this, if at all possible, because a hearing is a formal affair, it has rules with which you are not familiar, and it may not get you the result you want.

Sample 6
ORDER

ORDER

Court File No. **1**_____

Court Location ____**2**____

In the Provincial Court of British Columbia

In the case between:

3
_____

APPLICANT

and

4
_____

RESPONDENT

ORDER

BEFORE THE HONOURABLE JUDGE)   the_____**6**____day of

_____**5**_____)   _____, 20_____.

7 On application   [ ]   without a hearing

                       [ ]   after a hearing at_____on_____, 20_____.

And on the Court being advised that the name and birth date of each child is:

[Names of children]		[Birth dates of children]		
		M	D	Y
8_____		____	____	____
_____		____	____	____
_____		____	____	____
_____		____	____	____
_____		____	____	____

[ ] Interim Order   [ ] Final Order   [ ] By Consent   [ ] Without notice
to others (ex parte)

THIS COURT ORDERS THAT:

9 1.   The Applicant/Respondent shall have custody and guardianship of the children of the marriage.

(or)

1.   The parties shall have joint custody and guardianship of the children of the marriage and the children shall live primarily with the Applicant/Respondent.

SELF-COUNSEL PRESS — FCBC (6-1)03

Step Seven: The Order

Once you have reached a settlement, the judge will make an order. He will say, "I order that … ." Make a note of what the judge says. It will be your obligation to produce an order that corresponds with what the judge decides. See Sample 6 and use the parts that apply to your situation.

Take the completed order to the court registry. They will check it and have it signed and will provide you with a copy. You should make an extra copy and send it to the other party.

INSTRUCTIONS FOR SAMPLE 6

1 **Court File No:** Fill in the court file number, if you know it. If you do not know the number, the court registry will fill it in when you file the form.

2 **Court Location:** Insert the name of the city in which the order is being filed; i.e., Vancouver, Vernon, Victoria, etc.

3 **Applicant's name:** Insert your full legal name.

4 **Respondent's name:** Insert the other party's full legal name.

5 **Judge's name:** Fill in the judge's name. If you did not get the judge's name, ask at the registry or ask the clerk of the court at a break in the proceedings. They will give you the name. You use only the judge's surname.

6 **Date:** Fill in the day, month, and year the order was made.

7 **On application:** Check the box that applies to what the judge ordered. If you do have to go to a hearing, fill in the place and date of the hearing.

8 **Names of children:** Fill in the full legal names of the children and their dates of birth. Check the box that applies to your situation.

9 **Court orders:** Remove or add the correct information to this section. For example, "The Applicant shall have custody and guardianship of the children of the marriage."

10 2.   The Applicant/Respondent shall have reasonable access to the children of the marriage.

(or)

2.   The Applicant/Respondent shall have the following access to the children of the marriage:

_____

_____

_____

_____

3.   Upon the Applicant/Respondent having been found to have an income of $ **11**
the Applicant/Respondent shall pay to the Applicant/Respondent the sum of $_____ **12**
per month for the support of the children, payable on the 1st day of each month commencing on the
1st day of_____ **13** _____, 20_____ and continuing until the child is no longer a child as defined
in the Family Relations Act.

_____ **14**
By the Court

SELF-COUNSEL PRESS — FCBC (6-2)03

Instructions for Sample 6 — continued

10 **Access:** Remove or add the correct information for this section. For example, "The Respondent shall have reasonable access to the children of the marriage." Or you can fill in the amount of access the Respondent or Applicant has to the children.

11 **Income:** Strike through either the Applicant or the Respondent and insert the yearly income.

12 **Amount per month:** Strike through either the Applicant or Respondent and insert the monthly sum that will be paid for the support of the children each month.

13 **Date:** Insert the date that the payments will begin.

14 **Signature:** The judge or other registry personnel will sign the order after you hand it in to them and before you get it back.

5
Filing a Financial Statement

Step Eight: Financial Statement

You will need to file a financial statement if one or more of the following applies to you:

- There is a claim for spousal or parental maintenance.

- You are the person being asked to pay maintenance.

- The claim is for an amount other than the amount set out in the tables of the Child Support Guidelines (see Appendix 1).

- There is a claim of undue hardship.

- There is a claim for special or extraordinary expenses. If you have a special expenses claim, you will have to file a financial statement outlining your income and expenses because the special expenses will be apportioned between the two of you based on your relative incomes.

- The parents have split custody. This means there are two or more children and each parent has sole custody of a child not less than 40 percent of the time over the course of a year.

- One or more of the children for whom maintenance is claimed is of the age of majority (19 years in BC) or older.

- The person who is being asked to pay is not a biological or adoptive parent of the child but has acted as a parent to one or more of the children for whom maintenance is claimed.

See Sample 7 if you fall into one or more of the categories listed above.

Sample 7
FINANCIAL STATEMENT

Form 4 (Rule 4)

FINANCIAL STATEMENT

Court File No. **1**

Court Location **2**

In the Provincial Court of British Columbia

In the case between:

_____ **3** _____

(Applicant's name)

and **4**

_____

(Respondent's name)

_____

5 I,_____

(name)

Address for service_____City_____

Province_____Postal Code_____Phone_____Fax_____swear or affirm that:

1. The information set out in this financial statement is true, to the best of my knowledge.

2. I have made complete disclosure in this financial statement of - (check applicable boxes)

   6 [   ] my income, including benefits and adjustments, if any, in Part 1,

   [   ] my expenses, in Part 2,

   [   ] my assets and debts, in Part 3.

7 3. [   ] I do not anticipate any significant changes in the information set out in this financial statement.

Or

[   ] I anticipate the following significant changes in the information set out in this financial statement:

_____

_____

_____

8 SWORN OR AFFIRMED BEFORE ME   )

at_____, British Columbia)

(city, town, municipality)

on_____   )   _____

(date)

_____

A commissioner for taking affidavits
for British Columbia

INSTRUCTIONS FOR SAMPLE 7

1   **Court File No:** Fill in the court file number, if you know it. If do not know the number, the court registry will fill it in when you file the form.

2   **Court Location:** Insert the name of the city in which you are making the application; i.e., Vancouver, Vernon, Prince George, etc.

3   **Applicant's name:** Insert your full legal name.

4   **Respondent's name:** Insert the other party's full legal name.

5   **Name:** Insert your full legal name, address, telephone number, and fax number (if you have one).

6   **Parts:** Check the boxes beside the sections of the form that apply.

7   **Changes:** If your income last year, your income this year, and your expected income next year are all more or less the same, check the box that says, "I do not anticipate any significant changes." If you expect your income in the future to be substantially more or substantially less than it has been in the past, check the box that says, "I anticipate the following significant changes." Insert a brief explanation of the changes you anticipate.

8   **Sworn:** You must have it signed in front of a lawyer, a notary public, or a commissioner for taking affidavits. The charge will be in the range of $30 to $50.

For the purposes of this form:

"Social assistance" includes:

(a) Income assistance within the meaning of the BC Benefits (Income Assistance) Act,

(b) a youth allowance within the meaning of the BC Benefits (Youth Works) Act, and

(c) a disability allowance within the meaning of the Disability Benefits Program Act.

"Support" includes maintenance.

PART 1 INCOME

Complete Part 1 if —

(a) there is a claim, either by you or against you, for spousal or parental support; or

(b) there is a claim, either by you or against you, for child support and you are required by the Child Support Guidelines to provide income information.

9 1. I am

[ ] employed as_____

(describe occupation)

by_____

(name and address of employer)

[ ] self-employed_____

(name and address of business)

[ ] unemployed since_____

(month, day, year)

10 2. I am paid

[ ] every 2 weeks   [ ] twice a month   [ ] monthly

[ ] other *(specify)*_____

11 3. I have attached a copy of each of the applicable documents to my financial statement: *(check applicable boxes)*

[ ] every personal income tax return I have filed for each of the three most recent taxation years, together with any attachments

[ ] every income tax notice of assessment or reassessment I have received for each of the three most recent taxation years

[ ] **(if you are an employee)** my most recent statement of earnings indicating the total earnings paid in the year to date, including overtime, or where such a statement is not provided by my employer, a letter from my employer setting out that information, including my rate of annual salary or remuneration

[ ] **(if you are receiving Employment Insurance benefits)** my three most recent EIC benefit statements

[ ] **(if you are receiving Worker's Compensation benefits)** my three most recent WCB benefit statements

[ ] **(if you are receiving Social Assistance)** a statement confirming the amount that I receive

[ ] **(if you are self-employed)** for the three most recent taxation years

(i) the financial statements of my business or professional practice, other than a partnership; and

(ii) a statement showing a breakdown of all salaries, wages, management fees, or other payments or benefits paid to, or on behalf of, persons or corporations with whom I do not deal at arm's length

[ ] **(if you are a partner in a partnership)** confirmation of my income and draw from, and capital in, the partnership for its three most recent taxation years

[ ] **(if you control a corporation)** for its three most recent taxation years

(i) the financial statements of the corporation and its subsidiaries; and

(ii) a statement showing a breakdown of all salaries, wages, management fees, or other payments or benefits paid to, or on behalf of, persons or corporations with whom the corporation and every related corporation does not deal at arm's length

[ ] **(if you are a beneficiary under a trust)** the trust settlement agreement and the trust's three most recent financial statements

SELF-COUNSEL PRESS — FCBC (7-2)03

Instructions for Sample 7 — continued

9   **Employment:** Check the box that describes your employment situation. If you are employed or self-employed, fill in the name and address of your employer or business. If you are unemployed, fill in the month, day, and year of when you became unemployed.

10   **Pay period:** Check the proper box.

11   **Attachments:** Read this section carefully. Check all the boxes that apply to you. You will be expected to check at least the first two boxes and to attach your tax returns and notices of assessment. The notice of assessment is the form that Revenue Canada returns to you confirming that you have filed a tax return and that they have accepted the numbers in it. Some of the other boxes will apply to you and you will need to attach the documentation requested in each.

12 ANNUAL INCOME

*If line 150 (total income) of your most recent federal income tax return sets out what you expect your income to be for this year, skip to total income (line A) and record the amount from line 150 on line A. Otherwise, record what you expect your income for this year to be from each source of income that applies to you. Record gross **annual** amounts unless otherwise stated.*

1	Employment income *(include wages, salaries, commissions, bonuses, tips, and overtime)*		+ $_____
2	Other employment income		+ $_____
3	Pension income *(include CPP, Old Age Security, disability, superannuation, and other pensions)*		+ $_____
4	Employment insurance benefits		+ $_____
5	Taxable dividends from Canadian corporations		+ $_____
6	Interest and other investment income		+ $_____
7	**Net** partnership income: limited or non-active partners only		+ $_____
8	Rental income Gross $_____	**Net**	+ $_____
9	Taxable capital gains		+ $_____

10 Child support:

(a)	Total amount for children from another relationship or marriage	a. $_____*	
(b)	Total amount for children from this relationship or marriage	b. $_____*	
(c)	Taxable amount for children from another relationship or marriage	c.	+ $_____
(d)	Taxable amount for children from this relationship or marriage	d.	+ $_____

11 Spousal support:

(a)	From another relationship or marriage	a.	+ $_____
(b)	From this relationship or marriage	b.	+ $_____

12	Registered retirement savings plan income		+ $_____
13	Other income: *(include any taxable income that is not included on lines 1 to 17)*		+ $_____
14	**Net** self-employment income *(include business, professional, commission, fishing, and farming income)*		+ $_____
15	Workers' compensation benefits		+ $_____
16	Total social assistance payments		+ $_____
17	**Net** federal supplements		+ $_____
A	**Total income:**	**A =**	$_____

*Note: Do not add these items into the total at A.

SELF-COUNSEL PRESS — FCBC (7-3)03

Instructions for Sample 7 — continued

12 **Annual Income:** The purpose for this page of the financial statement is for you to disclose your current income. If your current income is the same as last year's income, all you need to do for this part of the form is move down to the line marked "A" and insert the gross income figure from your last year's tax return. It is at line 150 of your tax return.

13 **TOTAL BENEFITS**

List all allowances and amounts received and all non-monetary benefits from all sources that are not included in total income [line A]. You do not have to include here any Child Tax Benefit or BC Family Bonus that you receive for your children.

B Total benefits: B = $_____

14 **ADJUSTMENTS TO INCOME**

Complete this section if —

    (a) there is a claim, either by you or against you, for spousal or parental support; or

    (b) there is a claim, either by you or against you, for child support and you are required by the Child Support Guidelines to provide income information.

Deductions from Income:

1.   **Taxable** amount of child support I receive $_____

2.   Spousal support I receive from the other party $_____

3.   Union and professional dues   + $_____

4.   Other employment expenses *(Refer to* Schedule III *of the Child Support Guidelines)*

    Specify_____   + $_____

5.   Social assistance I receive for other members of my household and included in my total income   + $_____

6.   Dividends from taxable Canadian corporations

    (a) Taxable amount of dividends   a. $_____

    (b) Actual amount of dividends *(subtract)*   – b. $_____

    Excess portion of dividends (a–b)   = $_____ →+ $_____

7.   Actual business investment losses during the year   + $_____

8.   Carrying charges and interest expenses paid and deductible under the *Income Tax Act (Canada)*   + $_____

9.   Prior period earnings:

    (a) If net self-employment income included in total income includes an amount earned in a prior period, the amount earned in the prior period   a. $_____

    (b) Reserves *(subtract)*   – b. $_____

    Prior period earnings (a–b)   = $_____ →+ $_____

10.   Portion of partnership and sole proprietorship income required to be reinvested   + $_____

C   **Total deductions from income:**   C = $_____

Additions to Income:

1.   Capital gains

    (a) Actual capital gains   a. $_____

    (b) Actual capital losses *(subtract)*   – b. $_____

    (c) Taxable capital gains *(subtract)*   – c. $_____

    Total capital gains (a-b-c)   = $_____ → $_____

    (If amount is zero or less than zero, record "0" on this line)

SELF-COUNSEL PRESS — FCBC (7-4)03

Instructions for Sample 7 — continued

13 **Benefits:** This section is designed to have people who receive non-cash benefits in their income stream (such as car allowances and living out allowances) disclose these sources and amounts of income. For those of us who do not have that form of compensation in our income stream, this section will simply be left blank. If you do have this type of benefit payable to you on a regular basis, you should indicate the source and amount (or if you do not know an amount, at least the source and purpose).

14 **Adjustments:** If you receive taxable child support (that is child support payable on an order that existed since before the change making child support non-taxable), then include the annual amount at 1 if you have included that income in your total income amount on line A above. If you receive spousal support, include the annual amount at 2. If you pay union or other dues, include the annual amount(s) at 3. The essence of this section is that you are entitled to deduct from your annual income unearned items and items that do not belong to you personally but may have been included in your annual income amount on line A. For most of us, aside from the inclusion of union dues, this section will likely be left blank.

2.   Payments to family members and other non-arm's length persons

        (a) Salaries, benefits, wages, or other payments to family members or other non-arm's length persons, deducted from self-employment income   a. $____

        (b) Portion of payments necessary to earn self-employment income (*subtract*)   – b. $____

        Non-arm's length payments (a–b)   = $____ →+ $_____

3.   Allowable capital cost allowance for real property   + $_____

4.   Employee stock options in Canadian-controlled private corporations exercised

        (If some or all of the shares are disposed of in the same year you exercise the option, do not include those shares in the calculation.)

        (a) Value of shares when options are exercised   a. $____

        (b) Amount paid for shares (*subtract*)   – b. $____

        (c) Amount paid to acquire option to purchase shares (*subtract*)   – c. $____

        Value of employee stock options (a–b–c)   = $____ →+ $_____

D   **Total additions to income:**   **D =** $_____

15 **OTHER ADJUSTMENTS TO INCOME — Spousal or Parental Support**

(Complete this section only if there is a claim, either by you or against you, for spousal or parental support.)

1.   Total child support I receive $_____

2.   Social assistance I receive for other members of my household   + $_____

3.   Child Tax Benefit   + $_____

4.   BC Family Bonus   + $_____

E   **Total other adjustments:**   **E =** + $_____

16 **INCOME SUMMARY**

Annual Income for a Child Support Claim

Total income [from line A] $_____

(subtract)   Total deductions from income [from line C]   – $_____

(add)   Total additions to income [from line D]   + $_____

Annual income to be used for a Child Support Table amount   = $_____

(add)   Spousal support received from the other party (if any)   + $_____

(subtract)   Spousal support paid to the other party (if any)   – $_____

Annual income to be used for a special or extraordinary expenses claim   = $_____

Annual Income for a Spousal or Parental Support Claim

Total income [from line A] $_____

(subtract)   Total deductions from income [from line C]   – $_____

(add)   Total additions to income [from line D]   + $_____

(add)   Total other adjustments [from line E]   + $_____

Annual income to be used for a spousal or parental support claim   = $_____

Total Benefits [from line B]

SELF-COUNSEL PRESS — FCBC (7-5)03

15 **Other Adjustments:** This section applies only if you are making or defending a claim for spousal support. In the usual child support application, this section can be left blank. If you are dealing with a spousal support application, then fill in the amounts relative to 1 through 4. Some of them will be the same as what you entered in the previous section.

16 **Income Summary:** Insert the total income figure from line A.

17 **PART 2 EXPENSES**

You do not have to complete Part 2 if the only support claimed is child support in the amount set out in the Child Support Tables and all children for whom support is claimed are under the age of majority (19 years in BC).

ANNUAL EXPENSES

*Estimate your **annual** expenses:*

Compulsory deductions		Personal	
CPP contributions	$_____	Clothing	$_____
Employment insurance premiums	$_____	Hair care	$_____
Income taxes	$_____	Toiletries, cosmetics	$_____
Employee pension contributions to a	$_____	Education *(specify)*_____	$_____
Registered Pension Plan		Life insurance	$_____
Other *(specify)*_____	$_____	Dry cleaning/laundry	$_____
Housing		Entertainment, recreation	$_____
Rent or mortgage	$_____	Alcohol, tobacco	$_____
Property taxes	$_____	Gifts	$_____
Homeowner's/Tenant's insurance	$_____	Other *(specify)*_____	$_____
Water, sewer, and garbage	$_____	**Children ***	
Strata fees	$_____	Child care	$_____
House repairs and maintenance	$_____	Clothing	$_____
Other (specify)	$_____	Hair care	$_____
Utilities		School fees and supplies	$_____
Heat	$_____	Entertainment, recreation	$_____
Electricity	$_____	Activities, lessons	$_____
Telephone	$_____	Gifts	$_____
Cable TV	$_____	Insurance	$_____
Other *(specify)*_____	$_____	Other *(specify)*_____	$_____
Household expenses		**Savings for the future**	
Food	$_____	RRSP	$_____
Household supplies	$_____	RESP	$_____
Meals outside the home	$_____	Other *(specify)*_____	$_____
Furnishings and equipment	$_____	**Support payments to others**	
Other *(specify)*_____	$_____	*(specify)* **_____	$_____
Transportation		_____	
Public transit, taxis	$_____	_____	
Gas and oil	$_____	**Debt payments**	
Car insurance and licence	$_____	*(specify)*_____	$_____
Parking	$_____	_____	
Repairs and maintenance	$_____	_____	
Lease payments	$_____		
Other *(specify)*_____	$_____	**Other**	
Health		Charitable donations	
MSP premiums	$_____	Vacation	$_____
Extended health plan premiums	$_____	Pet care	$_____
Dental plan premiums	$_____	Newspapers, publications	$_____
Health care *(net of coverage)*	$_____	**Reserve for income tax**	$_____
Drugs *(net of coverage)*	$_____		
Dental care *(net of coverage)*	$_____		
Other *(specify)*_____	$_____	**F Total expenses**	**F = $_____**

* If you claim child support and special or extraordinary expenses, you must also complete Schedule 1.

** List only the names of those for whom support is not claimed in this application. Indicate whether the payments are tax deductible to you and whether you make the payments under a court order or agreement.

SELF-COUNSEL PRESS — FCBC (7-6)03

17 **Expenses:** If you are making a claim only for child support, you do not have to enter any information on this page. You may choose to do so as an exercise in budgeting but it is not necessary for a child support claim. If you are claiming spousal support, then you will have to complete the form. Please note that the figures to be inserted are annual rather than monthly. Note also that if you complete this section of the form, it must more or less equal your total income. For example, if you state that your annual expenses are $40 000.00 and your annual income is $20 000.00, the court is not going to be able to believe you unless you can explain how you spend twice as much as you have.

18 **PART 3 ASSETS AND DEBTS**

You do not have to complete Part 3 if the only support claimed is child support in the amount set out in the Child Support Guidelines and all children for whom support is claimed are under the age of majority (19 years in BC).

Assets

Real estate equity $_____

Market value $_____

Mortgage balance $_____

Other property:_____ + $_____

Cars, boats, vehicles   + $_____

Make and year:_____

      Market value   + $_____

      Loan balance   + $_____

      Pension plans   + $_____

Bank or other account *(include RRSPs)*   + $_____

Stocks and bonds   + $_____

Life insurance *(cash surrender value)*   + $_____

Money owing to me   + $_____

Name of debtor:_____

Other:_____ + $_____

(attach list if necessary)

G Asset value total   G = $_____

Annual debt payments

Credit card_____

Balance owing $_____

Date of last payment:_____

Reason for borrowing:_____

Bank or finance company_____

(do not include amount owing on mortgage)

Balance owing   + $_____

Date of last payment:_____

Reason for borrowing:_____

Department store_____

Balance owing   + $_____

Date of last payment:_____

Reason for borrowing:_____

Other *(attach list if necessary)*_____

Balance owing   + $_____

Date of last payment:_____

Reason for borrowing:_____

H Debt payment total   H = $_____

SELF-COUNSEL PRESS — FCBC (7-7)03

18 **Assets and Debts:** Fill in this section if you are making a spousal claim. If you have completed the expense section, you may also want to fill in this section.

   Note: These are annual figures and not monthly figures.

19 **SCHEDULE 1 – SPECIAL OR EXTRAORDINARY EXPENSES**

Complete if you claim special or extraordinary expenses as part of a child support claim.

Name of child:								
Child-care expenses	Gross $___	Net $___	Gross $___	Net $___	Gross $___	Net $___	Gross $___	Net $___
Medical/dental insurance premiums attributable to child	$___		$___		$___		$___	
Health related expenses (over $100)	Gross $___	Net $___	Gross $___	Net $___	Gross $___	Net $___	Gross $___	Net $___
Extraordinary expenses for primary or secondary school	$___		$___		$___		$___	
Post-secondary education expenses	Gross $___	Net $___	Gross $___	Net $___	Gross $___	Net $___	Gross $___	Net $___
Extraordinary extracurricular expenses	$___		$___		$___		$___	
Subtract contributions from child	$___		$___		$___		$___	
Total	$___		$___		$___		$___	

*To calculate the net amount, subtract from the gross amount subsidies, benefits, income tax deductions, or credits related to the expense. Give details below.

20 **SCHEDULE 2 — UNDUE HARDSHIP**

Complete if you plead undue hardship in respect of a child support claim.

Responsibility for unusually high debts reasonably incurred to support the family prior to separation or to earn a living:

Owed to: Terms of debt: Monthly amount
                                                                    $_____

Unusually high expenses for exercising access to a child:

Details of expense: Monthly amount
                                                                    $_____

Legal duty under a court order or separation agreement to support another person:

Name of person: Relationship: Nature of duty: Monthly amount
                                                                    $_____

Legal duty to support a child, other than a child for whom support is claimed in this application, who is: (a) under the age of majority (19 years in BC); or (b) the age of majority or over but unable to support himself or herself because of illness, disability, or other cause:

Name of person: Relationship: Nature of duty: Monthly amount
                                                                    $_____

Legal duty to support a person who is unable to support himself or herself because of illness or disability:

Name of person: Relationship: Nature of duty: Monthly amount
                                                                    $_____

Other undue hardship circumstances:

Details of other undue hardship circumstances: Monthly amount
                                                                    $_____

21 **SCHEDULE 3 - INCOME OF OTHER PERSONS IN HOUSEHOLD**

Complete this section if there is an undue hardship claim

Other person's name: Annual income
                                                    $_____
                                                    $_____

SELF COUNSEL PRESS — FCBC (7-8)03

19 **Special or Extraordinary Expenses:** If you are claiming something more than the basic amount of child support to compensate for special costs, then you need to complete this section. Child-care expense incurred in order to allow you to earn income is considered an extra expense. You can claim only the amount that you pay yourself. If you get compensation from the Government for these costs, you cannot claim them. Extra costs incurred to care for a disabled or difficult child are special costs. School expenses over and above normal ones are special expenses, as are tuition and costs for post-secondary education.

20 **Undue Hardship:** This section is to be filled in by the party against whom a claim is made. Where there are unusual debt costs, or where a child lives some distance away and it costs money to exercise access, the court has the power to reduce child maintenance below the table amount in the Child Support Guidelines. If you want the court to consider reducing the child maintenance, you must provide a complete breakdown of actual costs.

21 **Other Household Income:** This section is to be filled in only where there is an undue hardship claim. You must disclose the gross income of other people with whom you live and who work and have income to contribute to the household costs.

6
Protecting Yourself and Your Loved Ones

Step Nine: Restraining Order

If there has been violence in your relationship, or if you anticipate that the other party might be or may become violent and cause harm to you or to the children, you can ask the court for a restraining order. If you want a restraining order, you should have filled in Section 4 in the original application form (see Sample 1). In Section 4, you should have given a short explanation of why you feel a restraining order is necessary.

If you ask for a restraining order, the court will almost always grant one.

The form of the restraining order is as follows in Sample 8. Simply fill in the blanks and once you have done so, file the order in the court registry. If you are retyping the form using the form on disk, eliminate those provisions that do not apply to you. If you are using the form from the back of this book, simply cross off those provisions that do not apply to your situation.

Sample 8
RESTRAINING ORDER

Form 25 (Rule 18 (2) (A))
RESTRAINING ORDER

Court File No._____ **1** _____
Court Location_____ **2** _____

In the Provincial Court of British Columbia

In the case between:

_____ **3** _____
(name)

and _____ **4** _____
(name)

5 BEFORE THE HONOURABLE JUDGE) The_____day

_____) of_____, 20_____.

)

Persons appearing:_____ Lawyer:_____

_____ Lawyer:_____

[ ] Interim Order   [ ] Final Order   [ ] By Consent   [ ] Without notice to others (ex parte)

6 (if applicable) [ ] After a hearing at_____ the order dated_____ is
                                    (court location)   *(month, day, year)*
changed as stated below;

7 THIS COURT ORDERS THAT:

_____ is prohibited from entering
                    (name(s) of party(s))

any premises occupied by_____ or the children named below:
                                    (name of party)

Name(s) of child(ren)	Birth date(s) of child(ren)		
	mmm	dd	yyyy

or making contact with, or interfering with any of them, until further order of this court.

INSTRUCTIONS FOR SAMPLE 8

1   **Court File No.:** Fill in the court file number, if you know it. If do not know the number, the court registry will fill it in when you file the form.

2   **Court Location:** Insert the name of the city in which you are making the application; i.e., Vancouver, Vernon, Prince George, etc.

3   **Name:** Insert your full legal name.

4   **Name:** Insert the other party's full legal name.

5   **Court information:** Fill in the Judge's name, as well as the persons appearing and their lawyer's names. Also include the month, day, and year of the order. Check the applicable box.

6   **Changes to order:** This section applies only if your application is to change an existing order. If so, fill in the date of the original order, then go on with the remaining items.

7   **Names:** Fill in the name of the party prohibited from entering any premises occupied by you or the children. Enter your full legal name if you are the one being protected by the restraining order. If the restraining order is also protecting children, fill in their full legal names, and birth dates.

8 THIS COURT FURTHER ORDERS THAT:

_____
(name(s) of party(s))

[ ] pursuant to   [ ] s. 37 (a) F.R.A. or   [ ] s. 46 (a) F.M.E.A, is prohibited from molesting, annoying, harassing, or communicating with either_____or
(name of party)

the children named above, or attempting to molest, annoy, harass, or communicate with any of them;

[ ] pursuant to s. 38 (1) (a) F.R.A., is prohibited from entering a premises where the child(ren) named above reside from time to time;

[ ] pursuant to s. 38 (1) (b) F.R.A., is prohibited from making contact or endeavoring to make contact with or otherwise interfering with either the child(ren) named above or_____.
(name of party)

_____.

Further details of restraining order:

_____
_____
_____

9 (complete if applicable) [   ] Order to expire on_____
(month, day, year)

Checked by

10 Dated_____   _____   _____
(month, day, year)   *by the Court*   *Initials*

TAKE NOTICE THAT:

11 1. (a) Any peace officer including any RCMP officer having jurisdiction in the Province of British Columbia who finds the party_____breaching
(name of party(s))

any of the terms of this restraining order may immediately arrest that party **without warrant** pursuant to s. 495 (1) (b) of the *Criminal Code*, and may cause that person to be detained in custody, and to be taken before a justice to be dealt with according to law.

(b) Any peace officer including any RCMP officer having jurisdiction in the Province of British Columbia who on reasonable and probable grounds believes that the party_____
(name(s) of party(s))

_____ has, in the past, breached any of the terms of this restraining order may arrest that party **with a warrant** obtained pursuant to s. 26 of the *Offence Act*, and may cause that person to be detained in custody, and to be taken before a justice to be dealt with according to law.

8 **Additional Orders:** The restraining order you have obtained is made pursuant to section 37(a) of the Family Relations Act. Check that box and insert the name of the person who is restrained from contacting you and/or the children. If the order includes a prohibition from contacting children, check the two boxes that refer to section 38. If the order includes a prohibition from contacting anyone else (such as a boyfriend or some other family member), insert those names in the "name of party section" of the 38(1)(b) order. If there are any other prohibitions, write them out in the "further details" section.

9 **Order Expiration:** If the order is to expire, fill in the expiry date. An expiring order is unusual. You will most likely leave this section blank.

10 **Date:** Insert the date.

11 **Notice:** Insert the name of the party prohibited from contacting you in 1(a) and (b) at the bottom of the form and take the form to the registry for filing.

7
Other Applications

Step Ten: Out of Province Respondents

Often one of the parents lives in another province. If this is so in your case, there is a slightly different process to follow. You have two choices but both can be inefficient and take a long time.

You can go to the province where the other parent resides and commence the action there. The rules of another province's Family Court will be similar to British Columbia but not the same. This book will be of little use if you do go to another province to commence the action.

If the Respondent lives in another province and you want to start an action here, you must apply for a *provisional order*. This order is then sent by the registry to the other province where a hearing is held at which the Respondent can give his or her side of the story. The judge in the other province then issues an order, either on the terms of what the judge said in your province or on other terms based on whatever changes the Respondent's testimony necessitates.

The application is the same as set out in Step 1 (see Sample 1) except that in item 6 where you insert the Respondent's name and address you also insert in bold letters the phrase "EX PARTE" as follows:

Notice to: **EX PARTE**

(6) Name _____ Date of birth _____ (RESPONDENT)

Address for service _____ City _____

Province _____ Postal Code _____ Phone _____ Fax _____

Because this application will be made without notice to the other party, the court will not wait for 30 days for a reply. A date will be set for a hearing before the judge. At that hearing you must be prepared to give evidence. If the judge has the time to deal with the matter, then he or she will ask you to come forward and take the witness stand. If the judge does not have time to deal with the matter, then he or she will adjourn the matter to another date and you will have to attend court on that later date to give your evidence.

When your case is first called in Court stand up, identify yourself, and tell the judge you are asking for a provisional order. Once you take the stand, the clerk will ask you your name and likely will ask you to spell it. After that, it is up to you. Give the judge a short history of what has happened in your relationship. If the judge wants more information from you, he or she will ask for it. The following set of statements and questions are a guideline of what you might want to include in your short history:

- We were married *(when and where)*
- We have ____*(how many)* children.
- Their names and dates of birth are … .
- We separated *(when and where)*
- Since the separation, I have lived at *(place)* and the Respondent has lived at *(place)*.
- Who have the children lived with and where? For how long?
- What type of premises do you live in? What are the living and sleeping arrangements for the children?
- Where do the children attend school?
- How do you care for the children when you are not at home?
- Do you have extended family (i.e., parents/siblings) in the area and how involved are they in the children's lives?
- What do you do for a living? How much do you earn?
- What does the Respondent do for a living? What is your best estimate of what the Respondent earns and what do you base that estimate on?

The judge may then ask you more questions, and in the end, he or she will make an order. The registry staff will likely produce that order for you, but go to the registry after the hearing is over and make certain that they will.

The registry staff will send the order and a typed transcript of what you said during the hearing to the Court closest to where the Respondent lives. That court will issue a summons to the Respondent, and he or she will have to reply to it. Once that hearing has taken place, the court there will send a notification back to the issuing Court advising it of the result of the hearing. You will get a copy of that order. This process can take up to a year to complete.

Step Eleven: Ex Parte Applications

Where it is urgent or where you are having trouble finding the Respondent to serve him or her, the Court will grant interim orders without notice to the other side. These are called *ex parte* orders. That is simply a Latin phrase meaning *without notice*.

You will want to make an ex parte application when you have real grounds for a belief that the Respondent may react violently if you serve him or her with a normal application.

In this case, you file a normal application (see Sample 1) with the notation on it that it is ex parte. The process will be the same as in Step 10 above. However, as well as going through the evidence that is suggested in Step 10, you will also have to explain to the court why an ex parte order is necessary. The usual grounds for this are that the Respondent has threatened to harm you or to take the children from you if you take Court proceedings. You have to tell the judge this and you have to be specific.

In this case, the judge will issue what is called an interim or ex parte order. You will then be required to file that order and serve the application and the order on the Respondent (see Sample 4). The order that the judge grants will include a restraining order, so you will have to file a restraining order (see Sample 8).

You will want to make an ex parte application when you do not know where the Respondent is and cannot therefore tell a process server where to serve him or her with the Application.

The process is the same except in this case you need to tell the judge that you are asking for an order for "Substitutional Service." There are various orders that you can get. You can ask the judge for permission to serve a member of the Respondent's family, assuming that the notice will get through to the Respondent if served that way. You can ask for permission to serve his or her employer. Or you can ask for service by advertisement but that is very expensive and should only be considered as a last resort. The judge will want to use the method that will most likely result in the Respondent receiving notice of the application. Usually the application to serve some other family member is the best.

Step Twelve: Other Applications to the Court

At any time in the proceedings you can always go to court and ask the judge for assistance in solving any procedural problem or in dealing with any urgent matter that has arisen. To do that, you prepare and file a Notice of Motion (see Sample 9). The document should be prepared, filed, and served on the other party. There should be an affidavit in support of the motion filed with it outlining the circumstances that give rise to the application.

Sample 9
NOTICE OF MOTION

Form 16 (Rule 12 (1))
NOTICE OF MOTION

Court File No._____ **1**
Court Location_____ **2**
F.M.E.P. No._____

In the Provincial Court of British Columbia

In the case between:

3
_____
(name)

and

4
_____
(name)

_____

5 **Filed by:**

Name_____Date of birth_____
Address for service_____City_____
Province_____Postal Code_____Phone_____Fax_____

6 **Notice to:**

Name_____Date of birth_____
Address for service_____City_____
Province_____Postal Code_____Phone_____Fax_____

7 I,_____, will apply to this court at_____
   (name of person making application)   *(court location)*
on_____at_____a.m./p.m. for:
      (month, day, year)   *(time)*
[ ] Permission to file in the court registry at:_____
[ ] An order transferring this file to the court registry at:_____
[ ] An interim order under section 9 of the Family Relations Act as set out below.
[ ] A trial preparation conference.
[ ] An order cancelling a subpoena.
[ ] An order for the person named to produce records, as set out below.
[ ] An order for blood or tissue samples for paternity tests to be taken from the person named below.
[ ] Permission to use another service method, as set out below.
[ ] An order for service of_____ by a peace officer.
                              (name of document)
[ ] An order shortening or extending a "time limit," as set out below.
[ ] Directions on a procedural matter, as set out below.
[ ] An order for access to information under section 40 or 100 of the Family Relations Act.
[ ] An order settling the terms of an order.
[ ] An order changing as set out below, or cancelling, the attached order made in my absence.
[ ] Other order, as set out below.
Details of order(s) requested:_____
_____
_____

8 [ ] Any affidavits in support of this notice of motion are attached.

_____

Dated_____ **9** _____   Signature_____ **10** _____
      (month, day, year)

_____
Name lawyer of party bringing the motion

SELF-COUNSEL PRESS — FCBC (9-1)03

INSTRUCTIONS FOR SAMPLE 9

1   **Court File No:** Leave this space blank. When you take your completed form to the Court Registry, the clerk will fill in this number.

2   **Court Location:** Insert the name of the city in which you are making the application; i.e., Vancouver, Vernon, Prince George, etc.

3   **Applicant's name:** Insert your full legal name.

4   **Respondent's name:** Insert the other party's full legal name.

5   **Particulars of Applicant:** Enter your full legal name, address, telephone number, and fax number (if you have one).

6   **Particulars of Respondent:** Enter the other party's full legal name, address, telephone number, and fax number (if he or she has one). If there is an item that you don't know, just leave it blank.

7   **Particulars of the motion:** Fill in your full legal name, the court location, and the date. If you are using one of the forms from the back of this book, check the box that applies to you and cross out the lines that do not apply. If you are using the disk form, delete the lines that do not apply to your situation. Give details of the order(s) requested.

8   **Attached affidavits:** Check the box if any affidavits in support are attached.

    Note: The Notice of Motion should be prepared, filed, and served on the other party. There should be an affidavit in support of the motion filed with it outlining the circumstances that give rise to the application.

9   **Date:** Insert the month, day, and year.

10   **Signature:** Sign the application.

If All Else Fails

Step Thirteen: The Hearing

If you have gone through all the steps and still have not been able to re-solve matters, then you will have to have a hearing. This is what you have been trying to avoid by attempting to resolve the matter by agreement. In most cases, this step will not prove necessary.

A hearing is a trial but because it is in Family Court it is not subject to the stringent rules that usually apply to trials. If a hearing is necessary, the court will set a date for it and very likely will set a date prior to that for the parties to meet and discuss procedural matters including the exchange of documents and the determination of who will be witnesses. The approach that the Court takes is to have as much open disclosure between the par-ties as possible so that both sides know what to argue about and what not to argue about when the hearing commences.

The structure of a hearing is as follows:

1. The Applicant and the Applicant's witnesses give their evidence first. After each witness has finished, the Respondent is given an opportunity to cross-examine the witnesses as to their evidence.

2. The Respondent and the Respondent's witnesses give their evi-dence next. After each witness has finished, the Applicant is given an opportunity to cross-examine the witnesses as to their evidence.

3. The Applicant then is entitled to make a submission.

4. The Respondent then is entitled to make a submission.

5. The Court then renders a decision, either at that time or later on, in which case the judge simply says that he or she is reserving the decision. In the case of a reserved decision, the registry staff will send you a copy of the decision when the judge renders it. The judge makes almost all decisions immediately.

Look at Step 10. The guideline statements in Step 10 will give you an idea of how to proceed with your testimony and with the testimony of your witnesses. Think about what information each witness has that you want the Court to be aware of. Design a set of questions that will allow the witness to give answers that set out that information. For your own testimony, it makes sense to prepare a similar set of questions that you can answer, even though you will not be responding to questions. Having a predetermined set of questions will make it less likely that you will forget something of importance. Try to be thorough. This is the only chance you get to have your evidence placed before the Court and this will be the only evidence that the Court will have on which to base its decision.

The most important thing is to decide early on who it is that you will have as witnesses. You will be a witness, of course, and you will probably want to have as witnesses some members of your family or some friends who are familiar with your parenting abilities and skills. It is not likely that you will have anyone else.

Appendix 1
Child Support Tables for British Columbia

FEDERAL CHILD SUPPORT AMOUNTS : SIMPLIFIED TABLES   1997
MONTANTS FÉDÉRAUX DE PENSIONS ALIMENTAIRES POUR ENFANTS : TABLES SIMPLIFIÉES

Income/ Revenu ($)	Monthly Award/ Paiement mensuel ($) No. of Children/ Nᵇʳᵉ d enfants				Income/ Revenu ($)	Monthly Award/ Paiement mensuel ($) No. of Children/ Nᵇʳᵉ d enfants				Income/ Revenu ($)	Monthly Award/ Paiement mensuel ($) No. of Children/ Nᵇʳᵉ d enfants				Income/ Revenu ($)	Monthly Award/ Paiement mensuel ($) No. of Children/ Nᵇʳᵉ d enfants			
	1	2	3	4		1	2	3	4		1	2	3	4		1	2	3	4
6700	0	0	0	0	12000	99	157	179	201	17300	144	257	347	394	22600	198	337	449	542
6800	0	0	0	0	12100	99	160	183	205	17400	144	258	349	398	22700	199	339	451	544
6900	2	3	3	4	12200	99	163	186	209	17500	145	259	351	401	22800	200	340	453	546
7000	5	6	7	8	12300	99	166	189	212	17600	146	261	353	405	22900	201	342	455	549
7100	7	9	10	12	12400	99	169	192	216	17700	147	262	355	409	23000	202	343	457	551
7200	10	12	14	16	12500	99	172	196	220	17800	148	264	357	412	23100	203	345	459	553
7300	12	15	17	20	12600	100	175	199	223	17900	149	265	358	416	23200	204	346	461	556
7400	15	18	21	23	12700	101	177	202	227	18000	150	267	360	420	23300	205	348	463	558
7500	18	21	24	27	12800	102	180	206	231	18100	151	268	362	423	23400	206	350	465	560
7600	20	24	28	31	12900	103	183	209	235	18200	152	270	364	427	23500	207	351	467	562
7700	23	27	31	35	13000	104	186	212	238	18300	153	271	366	431	23600	208	353	469	565
7800	26	30	34	39	13100	105	189	215	242	18400	154	273	368	434	23700	209	354	470	567
7900	28	33	38	43	13200	106	192	219	246	18500	155	274	370	438	23800	210	356	472	569
8000	31	36	41	47	13300	107	195	222	249	18600	156	276	372	442	23900	211	357	474	572
8100	33	39	45	51	13400	108	198	225	253	18700	157	277	374	446	24000	212	359	476	574
8200	36	42	48	54	13500	109	200	229	257	18800	158	279	376	449	24100	213	361	478	576
8300	39	45	52	58	13600	110	203	232	261	18900	159	280	378	453	24200	214	362	480	578
8400	41	48	55	62	13700	111	205	235	264	19000	160	282	380	457	24300	214	364	482	581
8500	44	51	59	66	13800	112	207	239	268	19100	161	283	382	460	24400	215	365	484	583
8600	47	54	62	70	13900	113	208	242	272	19200	162	285	384	464	24500	216	367	486	585
8700	49	57	66	74	14000	114	210	245	275	19300	164	286	386	467	24600	217	368	487	587
8800	52	60	69	78	14100	115	211	248	279	19400	165	288	387	469	24700	218	370	490	590
8900	54	63	72	82	14200	116	213	252	283	19500	166	290	389	471	24800	219	371	492	592
9000	57	66	76	85	14300	117	214	255	287	19600	167	291	391	473	24900	220	373	494	594
9100	60	70	79	89	14400	118	216	258	290	19700	168	293	393	476	25000	221	375	496	597
9200	62	73	83	93	14500	119	217	262	294	19800	169	294	395	478	25100	222	376	498	599
9300	65	76	86	97	14600	120	219	265	298	19900	170	296	397	480	25200	223	378	500	601
9400	68	79	90	101	14700	121	220	268	301	20000	171	297	399	483	25300	224	379	502	603
9500	70	82	93	105	14800	122	222	271	305	20100	172	299	401	485	25400	225	381	504	606
9600	73	85	97	109	14900	123	223	275	309	20200	173	300	403	487	25500	226	382	506	608
9700	75	88	100	113	15000	124	225	278	313	20300	174	302	405	489	25600	227	384	508	610
9800	78	91	104	116	15100	125	226	281	316	20400	175	303	407	492	25700	228	386	510	613
9900	81	94	107	120	15200	125	227	284	320	20500	176	305	409	494	25800	229	387	512	615
10000	83	97	111	124	15300	126	229	287	323	20600	177	306	411	496	25900	230	389	514	617
10100	86	100	114	128	15400	127	230	291	327	20700	178	308	413	498	26000	231	390	516	619
10200	89	103	117	132	15500	128	232	294	330	20800	179	309	414	501	26100	232	392	518	621
10300	91	106	121	136	15600	129	233	297	334	20900	180	311	416	503	26200	233	393	520	624
10400	94	109	124	140	15700	130	234	300	337	21000	181	312	418	505	26300	234	394	521	626
10500	96	112	128	144	15800	131	236	303	341	21100	182	314	420	508	26400	234	396	523	628
10600	97	115	131	147	15900	131	237	306	344	21200	183	315	422	510	26500	235	397	525	630
10700	97	118	135	151	16000	132	239	309	348	21300	184	317	424	512	26600	236	399	527	632
10800	97	121	138	155	16100	133	240	312	351	21400	185	318	426	514	26700	237	400	529	634
10900	97	124	142	159	16200	134	241	316	355	21500	186	320	428	517	26800	238	402	531	636
11000	97	127	145	163	16300	135	243	319	359	21600	187	321	430	519	26900	239	403	533	638
11100	97	130	149	167	16400	136	244	322	362	21700	188	323	432	521	27000	240	405	534	640
11200	98	133	152	171	16500	137	245	325	366	21800	189	325	434	524	27100	241	406	536	643
11300	98	136	156	175	16600	138	247	328	369	21900	191	326	436	526	27200	242	408	538	645
11400	98	140	159	178	16700	138	248	331	373	22000	192	328	438	528	27300	242	409	540	647
11500	98	143	162	182	16800	139	250	334	376	22100	193	329	440	530	27400	243	411	542	649
11600	98	146	166	186	16900	140	251	337	380	22200	194	331	442	533	27500	244	412	544	651
11700	98	149	169	190	17000	141	252	341	383	22300	195	332	443	535	27600	245	413	545	654
11800	98	152	173	194	17100	142	254	343	387	22400	196	334	445	537	27700	246	415	547	656
11900	98	154	176	198	17200	143	255	345	390	22500	197	335	447	540	27800	247	416	549	658

Note: This table shows amounts of child support based on income to the nearest $100. There is a mathematical formula for calculating specific child support amounts between the $100 levels. For more information, please contact the Department of Justice.

Income/ Revenu ($)	Monthly Award/ Paiement mensuel ($) No. of Children/ N^{bre} d enfants 1	2	3	4	Income/ Revenu ($)	Monthly Award/ Paiement mensuel ($) No. of Children/ N^{bre} d enfants 1	2	3	4	Income/ Revenu ($)	Monthly Award/ Paiement mensuel ($) No. of Children/ N^{bre} d enfants 1	2	3	4	Income/ Revenu ($)	Monthly Award/ Paiement mensuel ($) No. of Children/ N^{bre} d enfants 1	2	3	4
27900	248	418	551	660	33200	289	483	637	761	38500	331	547	721	862	43800	375	615	808	966
28000	249	419	553	662	33300	290	484	638	762	38600	332	549	722	864	43900	376	617	810	968
28100	250	421	555	664	33400	291	485	640	764	38700	333	550	724	866	44000	376	618	811	970
28200	251	422	557	667	33500	292	486	642	766	38800	333	551	725	868	44100	377	619	813	972
28300	251	424	558	669	33600	292	487	643	768	38900	334	552	727	870	44200	378	621	815	974
28400	252	425	560	671	33700	293	489	645	770	39000	335	554	729	872	44300	379	622	816	976
28500	253	427	562	673	33800	294	490	646	772	39100	336	555	730	874	44400	380	623	818	978
28600	254	428	564	675	33900	295	491	648	774	39200	337	556	732	876	44500	381	625	820	979
28700	255	429	566	677	34000	295	492	650	776	39300	337	557	734	877	44600	381	626	821	981
28800	256	431	568	680	34100	296	493	651	777	39400	338	559	735	879	44700	382	627	823	983
28900	257	432	569	682	34200	297	495	653	779	39500	339	560	737	881	44800	383	628	825	985
29000	258	433	571	684	34300	298	496	654	781	39600	340	561	738	883	44900	384	630	826	987
29100	259	435	573	686	34400	299	497	656	783	39700	341	562	740	885	45000	385	631	828	989
29200	260	436	575	688	34500	299	498	657	785	39800	341	564	742	887	45100	386	632	830	991
29300	260	438	577	690	34600	300	499	659	787	39900	342	565	743	889	45200	386	634	831	993
29400	261	439	579	693	34700	301	501	660	789	40000	343	566	745	891	45300	387	635	833	995
29500	262	440	581	695	34800	302	502	662	791	40100	344	568	746	893	45400	388	636	835	997
29600	263	442	582	697	34900	302	503	663	792	40200	345	569	748	895	45500	389	638	836	999
29700	264	443	584	699	35000	303	504	665	794	40300	346	570	750	897	45600	390	639	838	1001
29800	264	444	585	700	35100	304	505	667	796	40400	346	571	751	899	45700	391	640	840	1003
29900	265	445	587	702	35200	305	507	668	798	40500	347	573	753	901	45800	391	641	841	1005
30000	266	446	588	704	35300	305	508	670	800	40600	348	574	755	903	45900	392	643	843	1007
30100	267	447	590	705	35400	306	509	671	802	40700	349	575	756	905	46000	393	644	845	1009
30200	267	448	591	707	35500	307	510	673	804	40800	350	577	758	907	46100	394	645	846	1011
30300	268	449	593	709	35600	308	511	674	806	40900	351	578	760	909	46200	395	647	848	1013
30400	269	451	594	711	35700	309	513	676	807	41000	351	579	761	911	46300	396	648	850	1015
30500	269	452	596	712	35800	309	514	677	809	41100	352	581	763	913	46400	396	649	851	1017
30600	270	453	597	714	35900	310	515	679	811	41200	353	582	765	915	46500	397	650	853	1019
30700	271	454	598	716	36000	311	516	681	813	41300	354	583	766	917	46600	398	652	855	1021
30800	272	455	600	717	36100	312	517	682	815	41400	355	584	768	918	46700	399	653	856	1023
30900	272	456	601	719	36200	313	519	684	817	41500	356	586	770	920	46800	400	654	858	1025
31000	273	457	603	721	36300	313	520	685	819	41600	356	587	771	922	46900	401	656	860	1027
31100	274	458	604	723	36400	314	521	687	821	41700	357	588	773	924	47000	401	657	861	1029
31200	274	459	606	724	36500	315	522	689	823	41800	358	590	775	926	47100	402	658	863	1031
31300	275	460	607	726	36600	316	524	690	825	41900	359	591	776	928	47200	403	660	865	1033
31400	276	462	609	728	36700	317	525	692	827	42000	360	592	778	930	47300	404	661	866	1035
31500	276	463	610	729	36800	317	526	693	829	42100	361	593	780	932	47400	405	662	868	1037
31600	277	464	612	731	36900	318	527	695	831	42200	361	595	781	934	47500	406	663	870	1039
31700	278	465	613	733	37000	319	529	697	833	42300	362	596	783	936	47600	406	665	871	1041
31800	279	466	615	735	37100	320	530	698	835	42400	363	597	785	938	47700	407	666	873	1042
31900	279	467	616	736	37200	321	531	700	837	42500	364	599	786	940	47800	408	667	875	1044
32000	280	468	618	738	37300	321	532	701	838	42600	365	600	788	942	47900	409	669	876	1046
32100	281	469	619	740	37400	322	534	703	840	42700	366	601	790	944	48000	410	670	878	1048
32200	282	471	621	742	37500	323	535	705	842	42800	366	603	791	946	48100	411	671	880	1050
32300	282	472	622	744	37600	324	536	706	844	42900	367	604	793	948	48200	411	672	881	1052
32400	283	473	624	745	37700	325	537	708	846	43000	368	605	795	950	48300	412	674	883	1054
32500	284	474	626	747	37800	325	539	709	848	43100	369	606	796	952	48400	413	675	885	1056
32600	285	475	627	749	37900	326	540	711	850	43200	370	608	798	954	48500	414	676	886	1058
32700	285	477	629	751	38000	327	541	713	852	43300	371	609	800	956	48600	415	678	888	1060
32800	286	478	630	753	38100	328	542	714	854	43400	371	610	801	958	48700	416	679	890	1062
32900	287	479	632	755	38200	329	544	716	856	43500	372	612	803	960	48800	416	680	891	1064
33000	288	480	634	757	38300	329	545	717	858	43600	373	613	805	962	48900	417	682	893	1066
33100	288	481	635	759	38400	330	546	719	860	43700	374	614	806	964	49000	418	683	895	1068

Income/ Revenu ($)	Monthly Award/ Paiement mensuel ($) No. of Children/ Nᵇʳᵉ d enfants				Income/ Revenu ($)	Monthly Award/ Paiement mensuel ($) No. of Children/ Nᵇʳᵉ d enfants				Income/ Revenu ($)	Monthly Award/ Paiement mensuel ($) No. of Children/ Nᵇʳᵉ d enfants				Income/ Revenu ($)	Monthly Award/ Paiement mensuel ($) No. of Children/ Nᵇʳᵉ d enfants			
	1	2	3	4		1	2	3	4		1	2	3	4		1	2	3	4
49100	419	684	896	1070	54400	463	753	985	1174	59700	499	813	1064	1269	65000	534	867	1133	1351
49200	420	685	898	1072	54500	464	754	986	1176	59800	500	814	1065	1270	65100	535	868	1135	1353
49300	421	687	900	1074	54600	465	755	988	1178	59900	500	815	1066	1272	65200	536	869	1136	1355
49400	421	688	901	1076	54700	465	757	990	1180	60000	501	816	1067	1273	65300	536	870	1137	1356
49500	422	689	903	1078	54800	466	758	991	1182	60100	501	817	1069	1275	65400	537	871	1139	1358
49600	423	691	905	1080	54900	467	759	993	1184	60200	502	817	1070	1277	65500	538	872	1140	1359
49700	424	692	906	1082	55000	468	761	995	1186	60300	502	818	1071	1278	65600	538	873	1141	1361
49800	425	693	908	1084	55100	469	762	996	1188	60400	503	819	1073	1280	65700	539	874	1143	1362
49900	426	695	910	1086	55200	470	763	998	1190	60500	504	820	1074	1281	65800	539	875	1144	1364
50000	426	696	911	1088	55300	470	764	1000	1192	60600	504	821	1075	1283	65900	540	876	1145	1366
50100	427	697	913	1090	55400	471	766	1001	1194	60700	505	822	1076	1284	66000	541	877	1147	1367
50200	428	698	915	1092	55500	472	767	1003	1196	60800	506	823	1078	1286	66100	541	878	1148	1369
50300	429	700	916	1094	55600	473	768	1005	1198	60900	506	824	1079	1287	66200	542	879	1149	1370
50400	430	701	918	1096	55700	474	770	1006	1200	61000	507	825	1080	1289	66300	543	881	1151	1372
50500	431	702	920	1098	55800	475	771	1008	1202	61100	508	826	1082	1291	66400	543	882	1152	1374
50600	431	704	921	1100	55900	475	772	1009	1204	61200	509	827	1083	1292	66500	544	883	1153	1375
50700	432	705	923	1102	56000	476	773	1011	1205	61300	509	828	1084	1294	66600	545	884	1155	1377
50800	433	706	925	1103	56100	477	774	1012	1207	61400	510	829	1085	1295	66700	545	885	1156	1378
50900	434	707	926	1105	56200	477	775	1014	1209	61500	511	830	1087	1297	66800	546	886	1158	1380
51000	435	709	928	1107	56300	478	776	1015	1211	61600	511	831	1088	1298	66900	547	887	1159	1382
51100	436	710	930	1109	56400	479	777	1017	1212	61700	512	832	1089	1300	67000	547	888	1160	1383
51200	436	711	931	1111	56500	479	779	1018	1214	61800	513	833	1091	1301	67100	548	889	1162	1385
51300	437	713	933	1113	56600	480	780	1020	1216	61900	514	834	1092	1303	67200	549	890	1163	1387
51400	438	714	935	1115	56700	480	781	1021	1218	62000	514	835	1093	1305	67300	549	891	1164	1388
51500	439	715	936	1117	56800	481	782	1022	1219	62100	515	837	1094	1306	67400	550	892	1166	1390
51600	440	717	938	1119	56900	482	783	1024	1221	62200	516	838	1096	1308	67500	551	893	1167	1391
51700	441	718	940	1121	57000	482	784	1025	1223	62300	516	839	1097	1309	67600	551	894	1169	1393
51800	441	719	941	1123	57100	483	785	1027	1225	62400	517	840	1098	1311	67700	552	895	1170	1395
51900	442	720	943	1125	57200	484	786	1028	1226	62500	518	841	1100	1312	67800	553	896	1171	1396
52000	443	722	945	1127	57300	484	787	1030	1228	62600	519	842	1101	1314	67900	553	897	1173	1398
52100	444	723	946	1129	57400	485	788	1031	1230	62700	519	843	1102	1316	68000	554	899	1174	1399
52200	445	724	948	1131	57500	486	789	1033	1231	62800	520	844	1104	1317	68100	555	900	1175	1401
52300	445	726	950	1133	57600	486	791	1034	1233	62900	521	845	1105	1319	68200	556	901	1177	1403
52400	446	727	951	1135	57700	487	792	1035	1235	63000	521	846	1106	1320	68300	556	902	1178	1404
52500	447	728	953	1137	57800	487	793	1037	1237	63100	522	848	1108	1322	68400	557	903	1180	1406
52600	448	729	955	1139	57900	488	794	1038	1238	63200	523	849	1109	1323	68500	558	904	1181	1408
52700	449	731	956	1141	58000	489	795	1040	1240	63300	523	850	1111	1325	68600	558	905	1182	1409
52800	450	732	958	1143	58100	489	796	1041	1242	63400	524	851	1112	1326	68700	559	906	1184	1411
52900	450	733	960	1145	58200	490	797	1043	1244	63500	525	852	1113	1328	68800	560	907	1185	1412
53000	451	735	961	1147	58300	491	798	1044	1245	63600	525	853	1115	1329	68900	560	908	1186	1414
53100	452	736	963	1149	58400	491	799	1046	1247	63700	526	854	1116	1331	69000	561	909	1188	1416
53200	453	737	965	1151	58500	492	800	1047	1249	63800	527	855	1117	1332	69100	562	910	1189	1417
53300	454	739	966	1153	58600	493	801	1048	1251	63900	527	856	1119	1334	69200	562	911	1191	1419
53400	455	740	968	1155	58700	493	802	1050	1252	64000	528	857	1120	1335	69300	563	912	1192	1421
53500	455	741	970	1157	58800	494	804	1051	1254	64100	529	858	1121	1337	69400	564	914	1193	1422
53600	456	742	971	1159	58900	494	805	1053	1256	64200	529	859	1123	1339	69500	564	915	1195	1424
53700	457	744	973	1161	59000	495	806	1054	1258	64300	530	860	1124	1340	69600	565	916	1196	1425
53800	458	745	975	1163	59100	496	807	1056	1259	64400	531	861	1125	1342	69700	566	917	1197	1427
53900	459	746	976	1165	59200	496	808	1057	1261	64500	531	862	1127	1343	69800	567	918	1199	1429
54000	460	748	978	1166	59300	497	809	1058	1263	64600	532	863	1128	1345	69900	567	919	1200	1430
54100	460	749	980	1168	59400	497	810	1060	1264	64700	532	864	1129	1347	70000	568	920	1202	1432
54200	461	750	981	1170	59500	498	811	1061	1266	64800	533	865	1131	1348	70100	569	921	1203	1434
54300	462	752	983	1172	59600	499	812	1062	1267	64900	534	866	1132	1350	70200	569	922	1204	1435

Income/ Revenu ($)	Monthly Award/ Paiement mensuel ($) No. of Children/ N^bre d enfants			
	1	2	3	4
70300	570	923	1206	1437
70400	571	924	1207	1438
70500	571	925	1208	1440
70600	572	926	1210	1442
70700	573	927	1211	1443
70800	573	928	1213	1445
70900	574	930	1214	1447
71000	575	931	1215	1448
71100	575	932	1217	1450
71200	576	933	1218	1451
71300	577	934	1219	1453
71400	578	935	1221	1455
71500	578	936	1222	1456
71600	579	937	1224	1458
71700	580	938	1225	1460
71800	580	939	1226	1461
71900	581	940	1228	1463
72000	582	941	1229	1464
72100	582	942	1230	1466
72200	583	943	1232	1468
72300	584	945	1233	1469
72400	584	946	1235	1471
72500	585	947	1236	1473
72600	586	948	1237	1474
72700	586	949	1239	1476
72800	587	950	1240	1477
72900	588	951	1241	1479
73000	589	952	1243	1481
73100	589	953	1244	1482
73200	590	954	1246	1484
73300	591	955	1247	1486
73400	591	956	1248	1487
73500	592	957	1250	1489
73600	593	958	1251	1490
73700	593	959	1252	1492
73800	594	961	1254	1494
73900	595	962	1255	1495
74000	595	963	1256	1497
74100	596	964	1258	1499
74200	597	965	1259	1500
74300	597	966	1261	1502
74400	598	967	1262	1503
74500	599	968	1263	1505
74600	600	969	1265	1507
74700	600	970	1266	1508
74800	601	971	1267	1510
74900	602	972	1269	1512
75000	602	973	1270	1513
75100	603	974	1272	1515
75200	604	975	1273	1516
75300	604	977	1274	1518
75400	605	978	1276	1520
75500	606	979	1277	1521

Income/ Revenu ($)	Monthly Award/ Paiement mensuel ($) No. of Children/ N^bre d enfants			
	1	2	3	4
75600	606	980	1278	1523
75700	607	981	1280	1524
75800	608	982	1281	1526
75900	608	983	1283	1528
76000	609	984	1284	1529
76100	610	985	1285	1531
76200	610	986	1287	1533
76300	611	987	1288	1534
76400	612	988	1289	1536
76500	613	989	1291	1537
76600	613	990	1292	1539
76700	614	992	1294	1541
76800	615	993	1295	1542
76900	615	994	1296	1544
77000	616	995	1298	1546
77100	617	996	1299	1547
77200	617	997	1300	1549
77300	618	998	1302	1550
77400	619	999	1303	1552
77500	619	1000	1305	1554
77600	620	1001	1306	1555
77700	621	1002	1307	1557
77800	621	1003	1309	1559
77900	622	1004	1310	1560
78000	623	1005	1311	1562
78100	624	1006	1313	1563
78200	624	1008	1314	1565
78300	625	1009	1316	1567
78400	626	1010	1317	1568
78500	626	1011	1318	1570
78600	627	1012	1320	1572
78700	628	1013	1321	1573
78800	628	1014	1322	1575
78900	629	1015	1324	1576
79000	630	1016	1325	1578
79100	630	1017	1327	1580
79200	631	1018	1328	1581
79300	632	1019	1329	1583
79400	632	1020	1331	1585
79500	633	1021	1332	1586
79600	634	1022	1333	1588
79700	635	1024	1335	1589
79800	635	1025	1336	1591
79900	636	1026	1338	1593
80000	637	1027	1339	1594
80100	637	1028	1340	1596
80200	638	1029	1342	1598
80300	639	1030	1343	1599
80400	639	1031	1344	1601
80500	640	1032	1346	1602
80600	641	1033	1347	1604
80700	641	1034	1349	1606
80800	642	1035	1350	1607

Income/ Revenu ($)	Monthly Award/ Paiement mensuel ($) No. of Children/ N^bre d enfants			
	1	2	3	4
80900	643	1036	1351	1609
81000	643	1037	1353	1611
81100	644	1039	1354	1612
81200	645	1040	1355	1614
81300	645	1040	1357	1615
81400	646	1041	1358	1617
81500	646	1042	1359	1618
81600	647	1043	1360	1619
81700	647	1044	1361	1621
81800	648	1045	1362	1622
81900	648	1046	1364	1624
82000	649	1047	1365	1625
82100	649	1047	1366	1626
82200	650	1048	1367	1628
82300	650	1049	1368	1629
82400	651	1050	1369	1631
82500	651	1051	1371	1632
82600	652	1052	1372	1634
82700	652	1053	1373	1635
82800	653	1054	1374	1636
82900	653	1054	1375	1638
83000	654	1055	1376	1639
83100	654	1056	1378	1641
83200	655	1057	1379	1642
83300	656	1058	1380	1643
83400	656	1059	1381	1645
83500	657	1060	1382	1646
83600	657	1061	1383	1648
83700	658	1062	1385	1649
83800	658	1062	1386	1650
83900	659	1063	1387	1652
84000	659	1064	1388	1653
84100	660	1065	1389	1655
84200	660	1066	1391	1656
84300	661	1067	1392	1658
84400	661	1068	1393	1659
84500	662	1069	1394	1661
84600	662	1070	1395	1662
84700	663	1071	1397	1664
84800	664	1072	1398	1665
84900	664	1073	1399	1667
85000	665	1074	1401	1668
85100	666	1075	1402	1670
85200	666	1076	1403	1671
85300	667	1077	1404	1673
85400	668	1078	1406	1674
85500	668	1079	1407	1676
85600	669	1080	1408	1677
85700	669	1081	1409	1679
85800	670	1082	1411	1680
85900	671	1083	1412	1682
86000	671	1084	1413	1683
86100	672	1085	1415	1685

Income/ Revenu ($)	Monthly Award/ Paiement mensuel ($) No. of Children/ N^bre d enfants			
	1	2	3	4
86200	673	1086	1416	1686
86300	673	1087	1417	1688
86400	674	1088	1418	1689
86500	675	1089	1420	1691
86600	675	1090	1421	1692
86700	676	1091	1422	1694
86800	676	1091	1423	1695
86900	677	1092	1425	1697
87000	678	1093	1426	1698
87100	678	1094	1427	1700
87200	679	1095	1429	1701
87300	680	1096	1430	1703
87400	680	1097	1431	1704
87500	681	1098	1432	1706
87600	682	1099	1434	1707
87700	682	1100	1435	1709
87800	683	1101	1436	1710
87900	684	1102	1437	1712
88000	684	1103	1439	1713
88100	685	1104	1440	1715
88200	685	1105	1441	1716
88300	686	1106	1443	1718
88400	687	1107	1444	1719
88500	687	1108	1445	1721
88600	688	1109	1446	1722
88700	689	1110	1448	1724
88800	689	1111	1449	1725
88900	690	1112	1450	1727
89000	691	1113	1451	1728
89100	691	1114	1453	1730
89200	692	1115	1454	1731
89300	692	1116	1455	1733
89400	693	1117	1457	1734
89500	694	1118	1458	1736
89600	694	1119	1459	1737
89700	695	1120	1460	1739
89800	696	1121	1462	1740
89900	696	1122	1463	1742
90000	697	1123	1464	1743
90100	698	1124	1465	1745
90200	698	1125	1467	1746
90300	699	1126	1468	1748
90400	699	1127	1469	1749
90500	700	1128	1471	1751
90600	701	1129	1472	1752
90700	701	1130	1473	1754
90800	702	1131	1474	1755
90900	703	1132	1476	1757
91000	703	1133	1477	1758
91100	704	1134	1478	1760
91200	705	1135	1480	1761
91300	705	1136	1481	1763
91400	706	1137	1482	1764

Income/ Revenu ($)	Monthly Award/ Paiement mensuel ($) No. of Children/ N^{bre} d enfants				Income/ Revenu ($)	Monthly Award/ Paiement mensuel ($) No. of Children/ N^{bre} d enfants				Income/ Revenu ($)	Monthly Award/ Paiement mensuel ($) No. of Children/ N^{bre} d enfants				Income/ Revenu ($)	Monthly Award/ Paiement mensuel ($) No. of Children/ N^{bre} d enfants			
	1	2	3	4		1	2	3	4		1	2	3	4		1	2	3	4
91500	706	1138	1483	1766	96800	740	1191	1551	1846	102100	774	1243	1618	1925	107400	808	1295	1686	2005
91600	707	1139	1485	1767	96900	741	1191	1552	1847	102200	775	1244	1620	1927	107500	808	1296	1687	2007
91700	708	1140	1486	1769	97000	741	1192	1553	1849	102300	775	1245	1621	1928	107600	809	1297	1688	2008
91800	708	1141	1487	1770	97100	742	1193	1555	1850	102400	776	1246	1622	1930	107700	810	1298	1690	2010
91900	709	1142	1488	1772	97200	743	1194	1556	1852	102500	776	1247	1623	1931	107800	810	1299	1691	2011
92000	710	1143	1490	1773	97300	743	1195	1557	1853	102600	777	1248	1625	1933	107900	811	1300	1692	2013
92100	710	1144	1491	1775	97400	744	1196	1558	1855	102700	778	1249	1626	1934	108000	811	1301	1693	2014
92200	711	1145	1492	1776	97500	745	1197	1560	1856	102800	778	1250	1627	1936	108100	812	1302	1695	2016
92300	712	1146	1494	1778	97600	745	1198	1561	1858	102900	779	1251	1628	1937	108200	813	1303	1696	2017
92400	712	1147	1495	1779	97700	746	1199	1562	1859	103000	780	1252	1630	1939	108300	813	1304	1697	2019
92500	713	1148	1496	1781	97800	747	1200	1564	1861	103100	780	1253	1631	1940	108400	814	1305	1698	2020
92600	713	1149	1497	1782	97900	747	1201	1565	1862	103200	781	1254	1632	1942	108500	815	1306	1700	2022
92700	714	1150	1499	1784	98000	748	1202	1566	1864	103300	782	1255	1634	1943	108600	815	1307	1701	2023
92800	715	1151	1500	1785	98100	748	1203	1567	1865	103400	782	1256	1635	1945	108700	816	1308	1702	2025
92900	715	1152	1501	1787	98200	749	1204	1569	1867	103500	783	1257	1636	1946	108800	817	1309	1704	2026
93000	716	1153	1502	1788	98300	750	1205	1570	1868	103600	783	1258	1637	1948	108900	817	1310	1705	2028
93100	717	1154	1504	1790	98400	750	1206	1571	1870	103700	784	1259	1639	1949	109000	818	1311	1706	2029
93200	717	1155	1505	1791	98500	751	1207	1572	1871	103800	785	1260	1640	1951	109100	818	1312	1707	2031
93300	718	1156	1506	1793	98600	752	1208	1574	1873	103900	785	1261	1641	1952	109200	819	1313	1709	2032
93400	719	1157	1508	1794	98700	752	1209	1575	1874	104000	786	1262	1642	1954	109300	820	1314	1710	2034
93500	719	1158	1509	1796	98800	753	1210	1576	1876	104100	787	1263	1644	1955	109400	820	1315	1711	2035
93600	720	1159	1510	1797	98900	754	1211	1578	1877	104200	787	1264	1645	1957	109500	821	1316	1712	2037
93700	720	1160	1511	1799	99000	754	1212	1579	1879	104300	788	1265	1646	1958	109600	822	1317	1714	2038
93800	721	1161	1513	1800	99100	755	1213	1580	1880	104400	789	1266	1648	1960	109700	822	1318	1715	2040
93900	722	1162	1514	1802	99200	755	1214	1581	1882	104500	789	1267	1649	1961	109800	823	1319	1716	2041
94000	722	1163	1515	1803	99300	756	1215	1583	1883	104600	790	1268	1650	1963	109900	824	1320	1718	2043
94100	723	1164	1516	1805	99400	757	1216	1584	1885	104700	790	1269	1651	1964	110000	824	1321	1719	2044
94200	724	1165	1518	1806	99500	757	1217	1585	1886	104800	791	1270	1653	1966	110100	825	1322	1720	2046
94300	724	1166	1519	1808	99600	758	1218	1586	1888	104900	792	1271	1654	1967	110200	825	1323	1721	2047
94400	725	1167	1520	1809	99700	759	1219	1588	1889	105000	792	1272	1655	1969	110300	826	1324	1723	2049
94500	726	1168	1522	1811	99800	759	1220	1589	1891	105100	793	1273	1656	1970	110400	827	1325	1724	2050
94600	726	1169	1523	1812	99900	760	1221	1590	1892	105200	794	1274	1658	1972	110500	827	1326	1725	2052
94700	727	1170	1524	1814	100000	761	1222	1592	1894	105300	794	1275	1659	1973	110600	828	1327	1726	2053
94800	727	1171	1525	1815	100100	761	1223	1593	1895	105400	795	1276	1660	1975	110700	829	1328	1728	2055
94900	728	1172	1527	1817	100200	762	1224	1594	1897	105500	796	1277	1662	1976	110800	829	1329	1729	2056
95000	729	1173	1528	1818	100300	762	1225	1595	1898	105600	796	1278	1663	1978	110900	830	1330	1730	2058
95100	729	1174	1529	1820	100400	763	1226	1597	1900	105700	797	1279	1664	1979	111000	831	1331	1732	2059
95200	730	1175	1530	1821	100500	764	1227	1598	1901	105800	797	1280	1665	1981	111100	831	1332	1733	2061
95300	731	1176	1532	1823	100600	764	1228	1599	1903	105900	798	1281	1667	1982	111200	832	1333	1734	2062
95400	731	1177	1533	1825	100700	765	1229	1600	1904	106000	799	1282	1668	1984	111300	832	1334	1735	2064
95500	732	1178	1534	1826	100800	766	1230	1602	1906	106100	799	1283	1669	1985	111400	833	1335	1737	2065
95600	733	1179	1536	1828	100900	766	1231	1603	1907	106200	800	1284	1670	1987	111500	834	1336	1738	2067
95700	733	1180	1537	1829	101000	767	1232	1604	1909	106300	801	1285	1672	1988	111600	834	1337	1739	2068
95800	734	1181	1538	1831	101100	768	1233	1606	1910	106400	801	1286	1673	1990	111700	835	1338	1740	2070
95900	734	1182	1539	1832	101200	768	1234	1607	1912	106500	802	1287	1674	1992	111800	836	1339	1742	2071
96000	735	1183	1541	1834	101300	769	1235	1608	1913	106600	803	1288	1676	1993	111900	836	1340	1743	2073
96100	736	1184	1542	1835	101400	769	1236	1609	1915	106700	803	1289	1677	1995	112000	837	1341	1744	2074
96200	736	1185	1543	1837	101500	770	1237	1611	1916	106800	804	1290	1678	1996	112100	838	1342	1746	2076
96300	737	1186	1544	1838	101600	771	1238	1612	1918	106900	804	1291	1679	1998	112200	838	1343	1747	2077
96400	738	1187	1546	1840	101700	771	1239	1613	1919	107000	805	1292	1681	1999	112300	839	1344	1748	2079
96500	738	1188	1547	1841	101800	772	1240	1614	1921	107100	806	1292	1682	2001	112400	839	1345	1749	2080
96600	739	1189	1548	1843	101900	773	1241	1616	1922	107200	806	1293	1683	2002	112500	840	1346	1751	2082
96700	740	1190	1550	1844	102000	773	1242	1617	1924	107300	807	1294	1684	2004	112600	841	1347	1752	2083

Income/ Revenu ($)	Monthly Award/ Paiement mensuel ($) No. of Children/ N^bre d enfants				Income/ Revenu ($)	Monthly Award/ Paiement mensuel ($) No. of Children/ N^bre d enfants				Income/ Revenu ($)	Monthly Award/ Paiement mensuel ($) No. of Children/ N^bre d enfants				Income/ Revenu ($)	Monthly Award/ Paiement mensuel ($) No. of Children/ N^bre d enfants			
	1	2	3	4		1	2	3	4		1	2	3	4		1	2	3	4
112700	841	1348	1753	2085	118000	875	1400	1821	2165	123300	909	1453	1888	2244	128600	943	1505	1956	2324
112800	842	1349	1754	2086	118100	876	1401	1822	2166	123400	909	1454	1889	2246	128700	943	1506	1957	2326
112900	843	1350	1756	2088	118200	876	1402	1823	2168	123500	910	1455	1891	2247	128800	944	1507	1958	2327
113000	843	1351	1757	2089	118300	877	1403	1824	2169	123600	911	1456	1892	2249	128900	944	1508	1959	2329
113100	844	1352	1758	2091	118400	878	1404	1826	2171	123700	911	1457	1893	2250	129000	945	1509	1961	2330
113200	845	1353	1760	2092	118500	878	1405	1827	2172	123800	912	1458	1895	2252	129100	946	1510	1962	2332
113300	845	1354	1761	2094	118600	879	1406	1828	2174	123900	913	1459	1896	2253	129200	946	1511	1963	2333
113400	846	1355	1762	2095	118700	880	1407	1830	2175	124000	913	1460	1897	2255	129300	947	1512	1965	2335
113500	846	1356	1763	2097	118800	880	1408	1831	2177	124100	914	1461	1898	2256	129400	948	1513	1966	2336
113600	847	1357	1765	2098	118900	881	1409	1832	2178	124200	915	1462	1900	2258	129500	948	1514	1967	2338
113700	848	1358	1766	2100	119000	881	1410	1833	2180	124300	915	1463	1901	2259	129600	949	1515	1968	2339
113800	848	1359	1767	2101	119100	882	1411	1835	2181	124400	916	1464	1902	2261	129700	950	1516	1970	2341
113900	849	1360	1768	2103	119200	883	1412	1836	2183	124500	916	1465	1903	2262	129800	950	1517	1971	2342
114000	850	1361	1770	2104	119300	883	1413	1837	2184	124600	917	1466	1905	2264	129900	951	1518	1972	2344
114100	850	1362	1771	2106	119400	884	1414	1838	2186	124700	918	1467	1906	2265	130000	951	1519	1973	2345
114200	851	1363	1772	2107	119500	885	1415	1840	2187	124800	918	1468	1907	2267	130100	952	1520	1975	2347
114300	852	1364	1774	2109	119600	885	1416	1841	2189	124900	919	1469	1909	2268	130200	953	1521	1976	2348
114400	852	1365	1775	2110	119700	886	1417	1842	2190	125000	920	1470	1910	2270	130300	953	1522	1977	2350
114500	853	1366	1776	2112	119800	887	1418	1844	2192	125100	920	1471	1911	2271	130400	954	1523	1979	2351
114600	853	1367	1777	2113	119900	887	1419	1845	2193	125200	921	1472	1912	2273	130500	955	1524	1980	2353
114700	854	1368	1779	2115	120000	888	1420	1846	2195	125300	922	1473	1914	2274	130600	955	1525	1981	2354
114800	855	1369	1780	2116	120100	888	1421	1847	2196	125400	922	1474	1915	2276	130700	956	1526	1982	2356
114900	855	1370	1781	2118	120200	889	1422	1849	2198	125500	923	1475	1916	2277	130800	957	1527	1984	2357
115000	856	1371	1782	2119	120300	890	1423	1850	2199	125600	923	1476	1917	2279	130900	957	1528	1985	2359
115100	857	1372	1784	2121	120400	890	1424	1851	2201	125700	924	1477	1919	2280	131000	958	1529	1986	2360
115200	857	1373	1785	2122	120500	891	1425	1853	2202	125800	925	1478	1920	2282	131100	958	1530	1987	2362
115300	858	1374	1786	2124	120600	892	1426	1854	2204	125900	925	1479	1921	2283	131200	959	1531	1989	2363
115400	859	1375	1788	2125	120700	892	1427	1855	2205	126000	926	1480	1923	2285	131300	960	1532	1990	2365
115500	859	1376	1789	2127	120800	893	1428	1856	2207	126100	927	1481	1924	2286	131400	960	1533	1991	2366
115600	860	1377	1790	2128	120900	894	1429	1858	2208	126200	927	1482	1925	2288	131500	961	1534	1993	2368
115700	860	1378	1791	2130	121000	894	1430	1859	2210	126300	928	1483	1926	2289	131600	962	1535	1994	2369
115800	861	1379	1793	2131	121100	895	1431	1860	2211	126400	929	1484	1928	2291	131700	962	1536	1995	2371
115900	862	1380	1794	2133	121200	895	1432	1861	2213	126500	929	1485	1929	2292	131800	963	1537	1996	2372
116000	862	1381	1795	2134	121300	896	1433	1863	2214	126600	930	1486	1930	2294	131900	964	1538	1998	2374
116100	863	1382	1796	2136	121400	897	1434	1864	2216	126700	930	1487	1931	2295	132000	964	1539	1999	2375
116200	864	1383	1798	2137	121500	897	1435	1865	2217	126800	931	1488	1933	2297	132100	965	1540	2000	2377
116300	864	1384	1799	2139	121600	898	1436	1867	2219	126900	932	1489	1934	2298	132200	965	1541	2001	2378
116400	865	1385	1800	2140	121700	899	1437	1868	2220	127000	932	1490	1935	2300	132300	966	1542	2003	2380
116500	866	1386	1802	2142	121800	899	1438	1869	2222	127100	933	1491	1937	2301	132400	967	1543	2004	2381
116600	866	1387	1803	2143	121900	900	1439	1870	2223	127200	934	1492	1938	2303	132500	967	1544	2005	2383
116700	867	1388	1804	2145	122000	901	1440	1872	2225	127300	934	1493	1939	2304	132600	968	1545	2007	2384
116800	867	1389	1805	2146	122100	901	1441	1873	2226	127400	935	1493	1940	2306	132700	969	1546	2008	2386
116900	868	1390	1807	2148	122200	902	1442	1874	2229	127500	936	1494	1942	2307	132800	969	1547	2009	2387
117000	869	1391	1808	2149	122300	902	1443	1875	2229	127600	936	1495	1943	2309	132900	970	1548	2010	2389
117100	869	1392	1809	2151	122400	903	1444	1877	2231	127700	937	1496	1944	2310	133000	971	1549	2012	2390
117200	870	1392	1810	2152	122500	904	1445	1878	2232	127800	937	1497	1945	2312	133100	971	1550	2013	2392
117300	871	1393	1812	2154	122600	904	1446	1879	2234	127900	938	1498	1947	2313	133200	972	1551	2014	2393
117400	871	1394	1813	2155	122700	905	1447	1881	2235	128000	939	1499	1948	2315	133300	972	1552	2015	2395
117500	872	1395	1814	2157	122800	906	1448	1882	2237	128100	939	1500	1949	2316	133400	973	1553	2017	2396
117600	873	1396	1816	2159	122900	906	1449	1883	2238	128200	940	1501	1951	2318	133500	974	1554	2018	2398
117700	873	1397	1817	2160	123000	907	1450	1884	2240	128300	941	1502	1952	2319	133600	974	1555	2019	2399
117800	874	1398	1818	2162	123100	908	1451	1886	2241	128400	941	1503	1953	2321	133700	975	1556	2021	2401
117900	874	1399	1819	2163	123200	908	1452	1887	2243	128500	942	1504	1954	2322	133800	976	1557	2022	2402

Income/ Revenu ($)	Monthly Award/ Paiement mensuel ($) No. of Children/ Nbre d enfants				Income/ Revenu ($)	Monthly Award/ Paiement mensuel ($) No. of Children/ Nbre d enfants				Income/ Revenu ($)	Monthly Award/ Paiement mensuel ($) No. of Children/ Nbre d enfants				Income/ Revenu ($)	Monthly Award/ Paiement mensuel ($) No. of Children/ Nbre d enfants			
	1	2	3	4		1	2	3	4		1	2	3	4		1	2	3	4
133900	976	1558	2023	2404	138000	1002	1598	2075	2465	142100	1028	1639	2127	2527	146200	1055	1680	2180	2589
134000	977	1559	2024	2405	138100	1003	1599	2077	2467	142200	1029	1640	2129	2529	146300	1055	1681	2181	2590
134100	978	1560	2026	2407	138200	1004	1600	2078	2468	142300	1030	1641	2130	2530	146400	1056	1682	2182	2592
134200	978	1561	2027	2408	138300	1004	1601	2079	2470	142400	1030	1642	2131	2532	146500	1057	1683	2183	2593
134300	979	1562	2028	2410	138400	1005	1602	2080	2471	142500	1031	1643	2133	2533	146600	1057	1684	2185	2595
134400	979	1563	2029	2411	138500	1006	1603	2082	2473	142600	1032	1644	2134	2535	146700	1058	1685	2186	2596
134500	980	1564	2031	2413	138600	1006	1604	2083	2474	142700	1032	1645	2135	2536	146800	1058	1686	2187	2598
134600	981	1565	2032	2414	138700	1007	1605	2084	2476	142800	1033	1646	2136	2538	146900	1059	1687	2189	2599
134700	981	1566	2033	2416	138800	1007	1606	2085	2477	142900	1034	1647	2138	2539	147000	1060	1688	2190	2601
134800	982	1567	2035	2417	138900	1008	1607	2087	2479	143000	1034	1648	2139	2541	147100	1060	1689	2191	2602
134900	983	1568	2036	2419	139000	1009	1608	2088	2480	143100	1035	1649	2140	2542	147200	1061	1690	2192	2604
135000	983	1569	2037	2420	139100	1009	1609	2089	2482	143200	1035	1650	2141	2544	147300	1062	1691	2194	2605
135100	984	1570	2038	2422	139200	1010	1610	2091	2483	143300	1036	1651	2143	2545	147400	1062	1692	2195	2607
135200	985	1571	2040	2423	139300	1011	1611	2092	2485	143400	1037	1652	2144	2547	147500	1063	1693	2196	2608
135300	985	1572	2041	2425	139400	1011	1612	2093	2486	143500	1037	1653	2145	2548	147600	1064	1693	2197	2610
135400	986	1573	2042	2426	139500	1012	1613	2094	2488	143600	1038	1654	2147	2550	147700	1064	1694	2199	2611
135500	986	1574	2043	2428	139600	1013	1614	2096	2489	143700	1039	1655	2148	2551	147800	1065	1695	2200	2613
135600	987	1575	2045	2429	139700	1013	1615	2097	2491	143800	1039	1656	2149	2553	147900	1065	1696	2201	2614
135700	988	1576	2046	2431	139800	1014	1616	2098	2493	143900	1040	1657	2150	2554	148000	1066	1697	2203	2616
135800	988	1577	2047	2432	139900	1014	1617	2099	2494	144000	1040	1658	2152	2556	148100	1067	1698	2204	2617
135900	989	1578	2049	2434	140000	1015	1618	2101	2496	144100	1041	1659	2153	2557	148200	1067	1699	2205	2619
136000	990	1579	2050	2435	140100	1016	1619	2102	2497	144200	1042	1660	2154	2559	148300	1068	1700	2206	2620
136100	990	1580	2051	2437	140200	1016	1620	2103	2499	144300	1042	1661	2155	2560	148400	1069	1701	2208	2622
136200	991	1581	2052	2438	140300	1017	1621	2105	2500	144400	1043	1662	2157	2562	148500	1069	1702	2209	2623
136300	992	1582	2054	2440	140400	1018	1622	2106	2502	144500	1044	1663	2158	2563	148600	1070	1703	2210	2625
136400	992	1583	2055	2441	140500	1018	1623	2107	2503	144600	1044	1664	2159	2565	148700	1071	1704	2211	2626
136500	993	1584	2056	2443	140600	1019	1624	2108	2505	144700	1045	1665	2161	2566	148800	1071	1705	2213	2628
136600	993	1585	2057	2444	140700	1020	1625	2110	2506	144800	1046	1666	2162	2568	148900	1072	1706	2214	2629
136700	994	1586	2059	2446	140800	1020	1626	2111	2508	144900	1046	1667	2163	2569	149000	1072	1707	2215	2631
136800	995	1587	2060	2447	140900	1021	1627	2112	2509	145000	1047	1668	2164	2571	149100	1073	1708	2217	2632
136900	995	1588	2061	2449	141000	1021	1628	2113	2511	145100	1048	1669	2166	2572	149200	1074	1709	2218	2634
137000	996	1589	2063	2450	141100	1022	1629	2115	2512	145200	1048	1670	2167	2574	149300	1074	1710	2219	2635
137100	997	1590	2064	2452	141200	1023	1630	2116	2514	145300	1049	1671	2168	2575	149400	1075	1711	2220	2637
137200	997	1591	2065	2453	141300	1023	1631	2117	2515	145400	1049	1672	2169	2577	149500	1076	1712	2222	2638
137300	998	1592	2066	2455	141400	1024	1632	2119	2517	145500	1050	1673	2171	2578	149600	1076	1713	2223	2640
137400	999	1593	2068	2456	141500	1025	1633	2120	2518	145600	1051	1674	2172	2580	149700	1077	1714	2224	2641
137500	999	1593	2069	2458	141600	1025	1634	2121	2520	145700	1051	1675	2173	2581	149800	1078	1715	2226	2643
137600	1000	1594	2070	2459	141700	1026	1635	2122	2521	145800	1052	1676	2175	2583	149900	1078	1716	2227	2644
137700	1000	1595	2071	2461	141800	1027	1636	2124	2523	145900	1053	1677	2176	2584	150000	1079	1717	2228	2646
137800	1001	1596	2073	2462	141900	1027	1637	2125	2524	146000	1053	1678	2177	2586					
137900	1002	1597	2074	2464	142000	1028	1638	2126	2526	146100	1054	1679	2178	2587					

Income/ Revenu ($)	Monthly Award/Paiement mensuel ($)			
	one child/ un enfant	two children/ deux enfants	three children/ trois enfants	four children/ quatre enfants
For income over $150,000	1079 plus 0.64% of income over $150,000	1717 plus 0.99% of income over $150,000	2228 plus 1.27% of income over $150,000	2646 plus 1.50% of income over $150,000
Pour revenu dépassant 150 000$	1079 plus 0,64% du revenu dépassant 150 000$	1717 plus 0,99% du revenu dépassant 150 000$	2228 plus 1,27% du revenu dépassant 150 000$	2646 plus 1,50% du revenu dépassant 150 000$

Appendix 2
Forms

This section contains blank copies of the sample forms used earlier in this book. You may tear out or photocopy any of the forms for your personal use only. Use the instructions for the Sample forms to help you fill in the blank forms. Read the instructions and the forms carefully and complete them according to your own situation. The forms are also provided on a 3½" disk; you may find it is easier to type in your information using the electronic versions of the forms.

Application to Obtain an Order (Form 1)

Application to Change or Cancel an Order (Form 2)

Affidavit in Support

Affidavit of Personal Service (Form 5)

Reply (Form 3)

Financial Statement (Form 4)

Restraining Order (Form 25)

Notice of Motion (Form 16)

Form 1 (Rule 2 (1))

APPLICATION TO OBTAIN AN ORDER

Court File No._____

Court Location_____

In the Provincial Court of British Columbia

In the case between:

_____

(Applicant's name)

and

_____

(Respondent's name)

Filed by:

Name_____Date of birth_____(APPLICANT)

Address for service_____City_____

Province_____Postal Code_____Phone_____Fax_____

Notice to:

Name_____Date of birth_____(RESPONDENT)

Address for service_____City_____

Province_____Postal Code_____Phone_____Fax_____

IMPORTANT NOTE TO RESPONDENT:

If this application contains a claim for maintenance, you are required to file financial information with your reply. If you do not, the court may attribute income to you and set the amount of maintenance to be paid. The applicant has estimated your gross annual income as set out in item 3 below.

I am applying for:

[ ] custody   [ ] guardianship   [ ] access

[ ] maintenance for a child   [ ] spousal maintenance   [ ] parental maintenance

[ ] an order prohibiting the respondent from interfering with the child(ren) and/or

_____

(name)

[ ] an order restraining the respondent from harassing the child(ren) and/or_____

_____

(name)

[ ] other order *(specify)*_____

1 — Orders and agreements

Are there any court orders or written agreements between the parties concerning separation, custody, access, or maintenance?

[ ] No orders   [ ] I am attaching copies of all other orders

[ ] No written agreements   [ ] I am attaching copies of all other written agreements

2 — Children *(complete if you are asking for custody, access, child maintenance, or a restraining order)*

Name(s) of child(ren)   Birth date(s)

_____

_____

_____

_____

_____

My relationship to the child(ren) is_____

The respondent's relationship to the child(ren) is_____

The present custody arrangements for the children are:_____

_____

(If applying for access) I am asking for access to the children as follows:_____

_____

_____

3 — Maintenance *(complete if you are asking for child or spousal maintenance)*

The current maintenance arrangements are:

_____

I believe that the respondent's gross annual income is $_____because

_____

_____

I am asking for: *(complete only if you are asking for child maintenance)*

[   ]   maintenance in the amount set out in the Child Support Table for_____children
         (number)

[   ]   special or extraordinary expenses, as follows:

       _____

       _____

Information for Applicant and Respondent

If this application contains a claim for maintenance, you must complete Form 4, following the instructions on that form, if —

- there is a claim for spousal or parental maintenance; or
- there is a claim for child maintenance and one or more of the following applies:
  - You are the person being asked to pay.
  - The claim is for an amount other than the amount set out in the tables of the Child Support Guidelines.
  - There is a claim of undue hardship.
  - There is a claim for special or extraordinary expenses.
  - The parents have split custody (that is, there are 2 or more children and each parent has sole custody of at least one child).
  - The parents have shared custody (that is, each parent exercises access to, or has physical custody of, a child for not less than 40% of the time over the course of a year).
  - One or more of the children for whom maintenance is claimed is of the age of majority (19 years in BC) or older.
  - The person who is being asked to pay is not a biological or adoptive parent of the child but has acted as a parent to one or more of the children for whom maintenance is claimed.

You may also provide this financial information before receiving the respondent's reply, in order to avoid delay, if you believe that the income of a respondent from whom child maintenance is claimed is over $150 000 per year, or that the respondent will claim undue hardship, special or extraordinary expenses, or make a counterclaim for maintenance.

4 — Restraining Orders *(complete if you are asking for a restraining order)*

I am asking for an order prohibiting the respondent from interfering with or harassing the children and/or myself because_____

_____

Note to respondent: If you fail to file a reply within 30 days of being served with this application, you will not receive notice of any part of the proceeding and the court may make an order against you.

Date_____   Signature_____
     (month, day, year)

APPLICATION TO CHANGE OR CANCEL AN ORDER

Court File No._____

Court Location_____

F.M.E.P. No._____

In the Provincial Court of British Columbia

In the case between:

_____

(Applicant's name)

and

_____

(Respondent's name)

Filed by:

Name_____Date of birth_____(APPLICANT)

Address for service_____City_____

Province_____Postal Code_____Phone_____Fax_____

Notice to:

Name_____Date of birth_____(RESPONDENT)

Address for service_____City_____

Province_____Postal Code_____Phone_____Fax_____

and to:

[ ] Director of Maintenance
Enforcement

[ ] Minister under the *BC Benefits (Income Assistance) Act*, the *BC Benefits (Youth Works) Act* or the *Disability Benefits Programs Act*

IMPORTANT NOTE TO RESPONDENT:

If this claim involves an order for maintenance, you may be required to file financial information with your reply. If you do not, the court may attribute income to you and set the amount of maintenance to be paid.

[   ] I ask that the attached order* dated_____be cancelled.
                                          (month, day, year)

Or

[   ] I ask that the attached order* dated_____be changed to the following:
                                          (month, day, year)

_____

_____

_____

Or

[   ] I ask that arrears of maintenance be cancelled or reduced as follows:

_____

_____

_____

Since the order dated_____was made, circumstances have changed as follows:
                         (month, day, year)

_____

_____

_____

Notice to respondent: If you fail to file a reply within 30 days of being served with this application, you will not receive notice of any part of the proceeding and the court may make an order against you.

Dated_____   Signature_____
       (month, day, year)

_____
     (name of applicant's lawyer)

*"Order" includes a written agreement filed under the Family Relations Act (section 121)

AFFIDAVIT IN SUPPORT

Court File No._____

Court Location_____

F.M.E.P. No._____

In the Provincial Court of British Columbia

In the case between:

_____

(Applicant's name)

and

_____

(Respondent's name)

AFFIDAVIT

I,_____, of_____in the Province of British Columbia

MAKE OATH AND SAY AS FOLLOWS:

1.   I am the Applicant in this proceeding.

2.   I have read the Application and the statements of fact made in it and verily believe that those statements of fact are true.

3.   I make this affidavit in support of my application to the Court.

SWORN BEFORE ME at_____   )

in the Province of British   )

Columbia this_____day of   )

_____, 20_____ .   )

)   _____

)   Applicant

)

_____   )

A Commissioner for taking affidavits

for British Columbia

Form 5 (Rules 2 (5) and 9 (10) (B))

AFFIDAVIT OF PERSONAL SERVICE

Court File No._____

Court Location_____

In the Provincial Court of British Columbia

I swear or affirm that I,_____, _____
  (name)   *(occupation)*

of_____personally served_____
                    (address)   *(name of person served)*

on_____at_____with a copy of the following document(s):
      (date)   *(address)*

(Make sure a copy of each document is attached and marked with the correct exhibit letter.)

Exhibit "A":_____
                                  (name of document)

Exhibit "B":_____
                                  (name of document)

The party served was identified to me in this manner:

[   ]   I know the person.

[   ]   He/She admitted to being this person.

[   ]   Other (specify)_____

SWORN OR AFFIRMED BEFORE ME   )

At_____, British Columbia   )
    (city, town, municipality)   )

on_____   )   _____
            (date)   *(signature)*

_____
A commissioner for taking affidavits
for British Columbia

Form 3 (Rule 3 (1) and (5))
REPLY

Court File No._____

Court Location_____

In the Provincial Court of British Columbia

In the case between:

_____
(name)

and

_____
(name)

To:

Name_____Date of birth_____(APPLICANT)
Address for service_____City_____
Province_____Postal Code_____Phone_____Fax_____

From:

Name_____Date of birth_____(RESPONDENT)
Address for service_____City_____
Province_____Postal Code_____Phone_____Fax_____

IMPORTANT NOTE TO APPLICANT:

If the respondent's reply includes a claim for maintenance, and you (the original applicant) do not file the required financial information with your reply, the court may attribute income to you and set the amount of maintenance to be paid. The respondent has estimated your gross annual income as set out in item 2 below.

Agreement with application:

I agree with the request(s) of the applicant for:

      [ ] custody   [ ] guardianship   [ ] access

      [ ] maintenance for a child   [ ] spousal maintenance   [ ] parental maintenance

      [ ] a change in or cancellation of an earlier order

      [ ] other order *(specify)*_____

I wish to make the following comments regarding the request(s) even though I agree:

_____

_____

_____

_____

_____

_____

Disagreement with application:

I disagree with the request(s) of the applicant for:

[ ] custody   [ ] guardianship   [ ] access

[ ] maintenance for a child   [ ] spousal maintenance   [ ] parental maintenance

[ ] a change in or cancellation of an earlier order

[ ] other order *(specify)*_____

I disagree because:

_____

_____

_____

_____

_____

Respondent's own application

I wish to make an application for the following:

[ ] custody   [ ] guardianship   [ ] access

[ ] maintenance for a child   [ ] spousal maintenance   [ ] parental maintenance

[ ] a change in or cancellation of an earlier order

[ ] an order that arrears under the *Family Relations Act* be cancelled or reduced

[ ] other order *(specify)*_____

1 — Children *(complete if you are asking for custody, access, or child maintenance)*

Name(s) of child(ren)   Birth date(s)

_____

_____

_____

_____

*(If applying for access) I am asking for access to the children as follows:*_____

_____

2 — Maintenance *(complete if you are asking for child or spousal maintenance)*

I believe that the applicant's gross annual income is $_____because_____

_____

3 — Restraining Order *(complete if you are asking for a restraining order)*

I am asking for an order prohibiting the applicant from interfering with or harassing the children and/
or myself because_____

_____

Dated_____   Signature_____

            (date)

ORDER

In the Provincial Court of British Columbia

In the case between:

_____

APPLICANT

and

_____

RESPONDENT

ORDER

BEFORE THE HONOURABLE JUDGE   )   the_____day of

_____   )   _____, 20_____.

On application   [   ]   without a hearing

                     [   ]   after a hearing at_____on_____, 20_____.

And on the Court being advised that the name and birth date of each child is:

[Names of children]	[Birth dates of children]		
	M	D	Y
_____	_____	_____	_____
_____	_____	_____	_____
_____	_____	_____	_____
_____	_____	_____	_____
_____	_____	_____	_____

[   ] Interim Order   [   ] Final Order   [   ] By Consent   [   ] Without notice to others (ex parte)

THIS COURT ORDERS THAT:

1.   The Applicant/Respondent shall have custody and guardianship of the children of the marriage.

(or)

1.   The parties shall have joint custody and guardianship of the children of the marriage and the children shall live primarily with the Applicant/Respondent.

2.   The Applicant/Respondent shall have reasonable access to the children of the marriage.

(or)

2.   The Applicant/Respondent shall have the following access to the children of the marriage:

_____

_____

_____

_____

3.   Upon the Applicant/Respondent having been found to have an income of $_____
the Applicant/Respondent shall pay to the Applicant/Respondent the sum of $_____
per month for the support of the children, payable on the 1st day of each month commencing on the
1st day of_____, 20_____ and continuing until the child is no longer a child as defined
in the Family Relations Act.

_____

By the Court

Form 4 (Rule 4)

FINANCIAL STATEMENT

Court File No._____

Court Location_____

In the Provincial Court of British Columbia

In the case between:

_____

(Applicant's name)

and

_____

(Respondent's name)

_____

I,_____

(name)

Address for service_____City_____

Province_____Postal Code_____Phone_____Fax_____swear or affirm that:

1. The information set out in this financial statement is true, to the best of my knowledge.

2. I have made complete disclosure in this financial statement of - (check applicable boxes)

     [   ]   my income, including benefits and adjustments, if any, in Part 1,

     [   ]   my expenses, in Part 2,

     [   ]   my assets and debts, in Part 3.

3. [   ]   I do not anticipate any significant changes in the information set out in this financial statement.

Or

     [   ]   I anticipate the following significant changes in the information set out in this financial statement:

     _____

     _____

     _____

SWORN OR AFFIRMED BEFORE ME   )

at_____, British Columbia)
 (city, town, municipality)

on_____   )   _____
          (date)

_____
A commissioner for taking affidavits
for British Columbia

For the purposes of this form:

> **"Social assistance"** includes:
>   (a) income assistance within the meaning of the BC Benefits (Income Assistance) Act,
>   (b) a youth allowance within the meaning of the BC Benefits (Youth Works) Act, and
>   (c) a disability allowance within the meaning of the Disability Benefits Program Act.
> **"Support"** includes maintenance.

PART 1 INCOME

Complete Part 1 if —

    (a) there is a claim, either by you or against you, for spousal or parental support; or
    (b) there is a claim, either by you or against you, for child support and you are required by the Child Support Guidelines to provide income information.

1. I am
    [ ] employed as_____
                       (describe occupation)

        by_____
                     (name and address of employer)
    [ ] self-employed_____
                     (name and address of business)
    [ ] unemployed since_____
                     (month, day, year)

2. I am paid
    [ ] every 2 weeks   [ ] twice a month   [ ] monthly
    [ ] other *(specify)*_____

3. I have attached a copy of each of the applicable documents to my financial statement: *(check applicable boxes)*

    [ ] every personal income tax return I have filed for each of the three most recent taxation years, together with any attachments

    [ ] every income tax notice of assessment or reassessment I have received for each of the three most recent taxation years

    [ ] **(if you are an employee)** my most recent statement of earnings indicating the total earnings paid in the year to date, including overtime, or where such a statement is not provided by my employer, a letter from my employer setting out that information, including my rate of annual salary or remuneration

    [ ] **(if you are receiving Employment Insurance benefits)** my three most recent EIC benefit statements

    [ ] **(if you are receiving Worker's Compensation benefits)** my three most recent WCB benefit statements

    [ ] **(if you are receiving Social Assistance)** a statement confirming the amount that I receive

    [ ] **(if you are self-employed)** for the three most recent taxation years
        (i) the financial statements of my business or professional practice, other than a partnership; and
        (ii) a statement showing a breakdown of all salaries, wages, management fees, or other payments or benefits paid to, or on behalf of, persons or corporations with whom I do not deal at arm's length

    [ ] **(if you are a partner in a partnership)** confirmation of my income and draw from, and capital in, the partnership for its three most recent taxation years

    [ ] **(if you control a corporation)** for its three most recent taxation years
        (i) the financial statements of the corporation and its subsidiaries; and
        (ii) a statement showing a breakdown of all salaries, wages, management fees, or other payments or benefits paid to, or on behalf of, persons or corporations with whom the corporation and every related corporation does not deal at arm's length

    [ ] **(if you are a beneficiary under a trust)** the trust settlement agreement and the trust's three most recent financial statements

ANNUAL INCOME

*If line 150 (total income) of your most recent federal income tax return sets out what you expect your income to be for this year, skip to total income (line A) and record the amount from line 150 on line A. Otherwise, record what you expect your income for this year to be from each source of income that applies to you. Record gross **annual** amounts unless otherwise stated.*

1 Employment income *(include wages, salaries, commissions, bonuses, tips, and overtime)*   + $_____

2 Other employment income   + $_____

3 Pension income *(include CPP, Old Age Security, disability, superannuation, and other pensions)*   + $_____

4 Employment insurance benefits   + $_____

5 Taxable dividends from Canadian corporations   + $_____

6 Interest and other investment income   + $_____

7 **Net** partnership income: limited or non-active partners only   + $_____

8 Rental income   Gross $_____   **Net**   + $_____

9 Taxable capital gains   + $_____

10 Child support:

   (a) Total amount for children from another relationship or marriage   a. $_____ *

   (b) Total amount for children from this relationship or marriage   b. $_____ *

   (c) Taxable amount for children from another relationship or marriage   c.   + $_____

   (d) Taxable amount for children from this relationship or marriage   d.   + $_____

11 Spousal support:

   (a) From another relationship or marriage   a.   + $_____

   (b) From this relationship or marriage   b.   + $_____

12 Registered retirement savings plan income   + $_____

13 Other income: *(include any taxable income that is not included on lines 1 to 17)*   + $_____

14 **Net** self-employment income *(include business, professional, commission, fishing, and farming income)*   + $_____

15 Workers' compensation benefits   + $_____

16 Total social assistance payments   + $_____

17 **Net** federal supplements   + $_____

A **Total income:**   A = $_____

*Note: Do not add these items into the total at A.

TOTAL BENEFITS

List all allowances and amounts received and all non-monetary benefits from all sources that are not included in total income [line A]. You do not have to include here any Child Tax Benefit or BC Family Bonus that you receive for your children.

B Total benefits: B = $_____

ADJUSTMENTS TO INCOME

Complete this section if —

    (a) there is a claim, either by you or against you, for spousal or parental support; or

    (b) there is a claim, either by you or against you, for child support and you are required by the Child Support Guidelines to provide income information.

Deductions from Income:

1.   **Taxable** amount of child support I receive $_____

2.   Spousal support I receive from the other party $_____

3.   Union and professional dues   + $_____

4.   Other employment expenses *(Refer to Schedule III of the Child Support Guidelines)*

    Specify_____   + $_____

5.   Social assistance I receive for other members of my household and included in my total income   + $_____

6.   Dividends from taxable Canadian corporations

    (a) Taxable amount of dividends   a. $_____

    (b) Actual amount of dividends *(subtract)*   – b. $_____

    Excess portion of dividends (a–b)   = $_____ →+ $_____

7.   Actual business investment losses during the year   + $_____

8.   Carrying charges and interest expenses paid and deductible under the *Income Tax Act (Canada)*   + $_____

9.   Prior period earnings:

    (a) If net self-employment income included in total income includes an amount earned in a prior period, the amount earned in the prior period   a. $_____

    (b) Reserves *(subtract)*   – b. $_____

    Prior period earnings (a–b)   = $_____ →+ $_____

10. Portion of partnership and sole proprietorship income required to be reinvested   + $_____

C   **Total deductions from income:**   C = $_____

Additions to Income:

1.   Capital gains

    (a) Actual capital gains   a. $_____

    (b) Actual capital losses *(subtract)*   – b. $_____

    (c) Taxable capital gains *(subtract)*   – c. $_____

    Total capital gains (a-b-c)   = $_____ → $_____

    (If amount is zero or less than zero, record "0" on this line)

2.   Payments to family members and other non-arm's length persons

     (a) Salaries, benefits, wages, or other payments to family members or other non-arm's length persons, deducted from self-employment income   a. $_____

     (b) Portion of payments necessary to earn self-employment income *(subtract)*   – b. $_____

     Non-arm's length payments (a–b)   = $_____ →+ $_____

3.   Allowable capital cost allowance for real property   + $_____

4.   Employee stock options in Canadian-controlled private corporations exercised

     (If some or all of the shares are disposed of in the same year you exercise the option, do not include those shares in the calculation.)

     (a) Value of shares when options are exercised   a. $_____

     (b) Amount paid for shares *(subtract)*   – b. $_____

     (c) Amount paid to acquire option to purchase shares *(subtract)*   – c. $_____

     Value of employee stock options (a–b–c)   = $_____ →+ $_____

D   **Total additions to income:**   **D =** $_____

OTHER ADJUSTMENTS TO INCOME — Spousal or Parental Support

(Complete this section only if there is a claim, either by you or against you, for spousal or parental support.)

1.   Total child support I receive $_____

2.   Social assistance I receive for other members of my household   + $_____

3.   Child Tax Benefit   + $_____

4.   BC Family Bonus   + $_____

E   **Total other adjustments:**   **E =** + $_____

INCOME SUMMARY

Annual Income for a Child Support Claim

Total income [from line A] $_____

(subtract)   Total deductions from income [from line C]   – $_____

(add)   Total additions to income [from line D]   + $_____

Annual income to be used for a Child Support Table amount   = $_____

(add)   Spousal support received from the other party (if any)   + $_____

(subtract)   Spousal support paid to the other party (if any)   – $_____

Annual income to be used for a special or extraordinary expenses claim   = $_____

Annual Income for a Spousal or Parental Support Claim

Total income [from line A] $_____

(subtract)   Total deductions from income [from line C]   – $_____

(add)   Total additions to income [from line D]   + $_____

(add)   Total other adjustments [from line E]   + $_____

Annual income to be used for a spousal or parental support claim   = $_____

Total Benefits [from line B]

PART 2 EXPENSES

You do not have to complete Part 2 if the only support claimed is child support in the amount set out in the Child Support Tables and all children for whom support is claimed are under the age of majority (19 years in BC).

ANNUAL EXPENSES

*Estimate your **annual** expenses:*

Compulsory deductions		**Personal**	
CPP contributions	$_____	Clothing	$_____
Employment insurance premiums	$_____	Hair care	$_____
Income taxes	$_____	Toiletries, cosmetics	$_____
Employee pension contributions to a	$_____	Education *(specify)*_____	$_____
Registered Pension Plan		Life insurance	$_____
Other *(specify)*_____	$_____	Dry cleaning/laundry	$_____
Housing		Entertainment, recreation	$_____
Rent or mortgage	$_____	Alcohol, tobacco	$_____
Property taxes	$_____	Gifts	$_____
Homeowner's/Tenant's insurance	$_____	Other *(specify)*_____	$_____
Water, sewer, and garbage	$_____	**Children ** *	
Strata fees	$_____	Child care	$_____
House repairs and maintenance	$_____	Clothing	$_____
Other (specify)	$_____	Hair care	$_____
Utilities		School fees and supplies	$_____
Heat	$_____	Entertainment, recreation	$_____
Electricity	$_____	Activities, lessons	$_____
Telephone	$_____	Gifts	$_____
Cable TV	$_____	Insurance	$_____
Other *(specify)*_____	$_____	*Other (specify)*_____	$_____
Household expenses		**Savings for the future**	
Food	$_____	RRSP	$_____
Household supplies	$_____	RESP	$_____
Meals outside the home	$_____	Other *(specify)*_____	$_____
Furnishings and equipment	$_____	**Support payments to others**	
Other *(specify)*_____	$_____	*(specify)* **_____	$_____
Transportation		_____	
Public transit, taxis	$_____	_____	
Gas and oil	$_____	**Debt payments**	
Car insurance and licence	$_____	*(specify)*_____	$_____
Parking	$_____	_____	
Repairs and maintenance	$_____	_____	
Lease payments	$_____	_____	
Other *(specify)*_____	$_____	**Other**	
Health		Charitable donations	
MSP premiums	$_____	Vacation	$_____
Extended health plan premiums	$_____	Pet care	$_____
Dental plan premiums	$_____	Newspapers, publications	$_____
Health care *(net of coverage)*	$_____	**Reserve for income tax**	$_____
Drugs *(net of coverage)*	$_____		
Dental care *(net of coverage)*	$_____		
Other *(specify)*_____	$_____	**F Total expenses** F =	$_____

*   If you claim child support and special or extraordinary expenses, you must also complete Schedule 1.

** List only the names of those for whom support is not claimed in this application. Indicate whether the payments are tax deductible to you and whether you make the payments under a court order or agreement.

PART 3 ASSETS AND DEBTS

You do not have to complete Part 3 if the only support claimed is child support in the amount set out in the Child Support Guidelines and all children for whom support is claimed are under the age of majority (19 years in BC).

Assets

Real estate equity	$_____
Market value	$_____
Mortgage balance	$_____
Other property:_____	+ $_____
Cars, boats, vehicles	+ $_____
Make and year:_____	
Market value	+ $_____
Loan balance	+ $_____
Pension plans	+ $_____
Bank or other account *(include RRSPs)*	+ $_____
Stocks and bonds	+ $_____
Life insurance *(cash surrender value)*	+ $_____
Money owing to me	+ $_____
Name of debtor:_____	
Other:_____	+ $_____
(attach list if necessary)	

G Asset value total　　　　　　　　　　G = $_____

Annual debt payments

Credit card_____

Balance owing	$_____

Date of last payment:_____

Reason for borrowing:_____

Bank or finance company_____

(do not include amount owing on mortgage)

Balance owing	+ $_____

Date of last payment:_____

Reason for borrowing:_____

Department store_____

Balance owing	+ $_____

Date of last payment:_____

Reason for borrowing:_____

Other *(attach list if necessary)*_____

Balance owing	+ $_____

Date of last payment:_____

Reason for borrowing:_____

H Debt payment total　　　　　　　　　H = $_____

SCHEDULE 1 – SPECIAL OR EXTRAORDINARY EXPENSES

Complete if you claim special or extraordinary expenses as part of a child support claim.

Name of child:								
Child-care expenses	Gross $____	Net $____	Gross $____	Net $____	Gross $____	Net $____	Gross $____	Net $____
Medical/dental insurance premiums attributable to child	$_____		$_____		$_____		$_____	
Health related expenses (over $100)	Gross $____	Net $____	Gross $____	Net $____	Gross $____	Net $____	Gross $____	Net $____
Extraordinary expenses for primary or secondary school	$_____		$_____		$_____		$_____	
Post-secondary education expenses	Gross $____	Net $____	Gross $____	Net $____	Gross $____	Net $____	Gross $____	Net $____
Extraordinary extracurricular expenses	$_____		$_____		$_____		$_____	
Subtract contributions from child	$_____		$_____		$_____		$_____	
Total	$_____		$_____		$_____		$_____	

*To calculate the net amount, subtract from the gross amount subsidies, benefits, income tax deductions, or credits related to the expense. Give details below.

SCHEDULE 2 — UNDUE HARDSHIP

Complete if you plead undue hardship in respect of a child support claim.

Responsibility for unusually high debts reasonably incurred to support the family prior to separation or to earn a living:

Owed to: Terms of debt: Monthly amount
$_____

Unusually high expenses for exercising access to a child:
Details of expense: Monthly amount
$_____

Legal duty under a court order or separation agreement to support another person:
Name of person: Relationship: Nature of duty: Monthly amount
$_____

Legal duty to support a child, other than a child for whom support is claimed in this application, who is: (a) under the age of majority (19 years in BC); or (b) the age of majority or over but unable to support himself or herself because of illness, disability, or other cause:
Name of person: Relationship: Nature of duty: Monthly amount
$_____

Legal duty to support a person who is unable to support himself or herself because of illness or disability:
Name of person: Relationship: Nature of duty: Monthly amount
$_____

Other undue hardship circumstances:
Details of other undue hardship circumstances: Monthly amount
$_____

SCHEDULE 3 - INCOME OF OTHER PERSONS IN HOUSEHOLD

Complete this section if there is an undue hardship claim

Other person's name: Annual income
$_____
$_____

Form 25 (Rule 18 (2) (A))

RESTRAINING ORDER

Court File No._____

Court Location_____

In the Provincial Court of British Columbia

In the case between:

_____

(name)

and

_____

(name)

BEFORE THE HONOURABLE JUDGE   )   The_____day

_____)   of_____, 20_____.

)

Persons appearing:_____Lawyer:_____

_____Lawyer:_____

[   ] Interim Order   [   ] Final Order   [   ] By Consent   [   ] Without notice to others (ex parte)

(if applicable) [   ] After a hearing at_____the order dated_____is

                                      (court location)   *(month, day, year)*

changed as stated below;

THIS COURT ORDERS THAT:

_____is prohibited from entering

                (name(s) of party(s))

any premises occupied by_____or the children named below:

                            (name of party)

Name(s) of child(ren)	Birth date(s) of child(ren)		
	mmm	dd	yyyy

or making contact with, or interfering with any of them, until further order of this court.

THIS COURT FURTHER ORDERS THAT:

_____
(name(s) of party(s))

[ ] pursuant to   [ ] s. 37 (a) F.R.A. or   [ ] s. 46 (a) F.M.E.A, is prohibited from molesting, annoying, harassing, or communicating with either_____or
(name of party)

the children named above, or attempting to molest, annoy, harass, or communicate with any of them;

[ ] pursuant to s. 38 (1) (a) F.R.A., is prohibited from entering a premises where the child(ren) named above reside from time to time;

[ ] pursuant to s. 38 (1) (b) F.R.A., is prohibited from making contact or endeavoring to make contact with or otherwise interfering with either the child(ren) named above or_____.
(name of party)

_____.

Further details of restraining order:

_____

_____

_____

(complete if applicable) [   ] Order to expire on_____
(month, day, year)

Checked by

Dated_____   _____   _____
(month, day, year)   *by the Court*   *Initials*

TAKE NOTICE THAT:

1. (a) Any peace officer including any RCMP officer having jurisdiction in the Province of British Columbia who finds the party_____breaching
(name of party(s))

any of the terms of this restraining order may immediately arrest that party **without warrant** pursuant to s. 495 (1) (b) of the *Criminal Code*, and may cause that person to be detained in custody, and to be taken before a justice to be dealt with according to law.

    (b) Any peace officer including any RCMP officer having jurisdiction in the Province of British Columbia who on reasonable and probable grounds believes that the party_____
(name(s) of party(s))

_____has, in the past, breached any of the terms of this restraining order may arrest that party **with a warrant** obtained pursuant to s. 26 of the *Offence Act*, and may cause that person to be detained in custody, and to be taken before a justice to be dealt with according to law.

Form 16 (Rule 12 (1))
NOTICE OF MOTION

Court File No._____
Court Location_____
F.M.E.P. No._____

In the Provincial Court of British Columbia

In the case between:

_____
(name)

and

_____
(name)

Filed by:

Name_____Date of birth_____
Address for service_____City_____
Province_____Postal Code_____Phone_____Fax_____

Notice to:

Name_____Date of birth_____
Address for service_____City_____
Province_____Postal Code_____Phone_____Fax_____

I,_____, will apply to this court at_____
    (name of person making application)   *(court location)*
on_____at_____a.m./p.m. for:
    (month, day, year)   *(time)*

[ ] Permission to file in the court registry at:_____
[ ] An order transferring this file to the court registry at:_____
[ ] An interim order under section 9 of the Family Relations Act as set out below.
[ ] A trial preparation conference.
[ ] An order cancelling a subpoena.
[ ] An order for the person named to produce records, as set out below.
[ ] An order for blood or tissue samples for paternity tests to be taken from the person named below.
[ ] Permission to use another service method, as set out below.
[ ] An order for service of_____ by a peace officer.
                       (name of document)
[ ] An order shortening or extending a "time limit," as set out below.
[ ] Directions on a procedural matter, as set out below.
[ ] An order for access to information under section 40 or 100 of the Family Relations Act.
[ ] An order settling the terms of an order.
[ ] An order changing as set out below, or cancelling, the attached order made in my absence.
[ ] Other order, as set out below.
Details of order(s) requested:_____
_____
_____

[ ] Any affidavits in support of this notice of motion are attached.

Dated_____   Signature_____
    (month, day, year)

_____
Name lawyer of party bringing the motion